Oklahoma
Native Plants
FOR PEOPLE AND POLLINATORS

Connie Scothorn, ASLA
with Brian Patric, ASLA

PRINTED IN THE UNITED STATES OF AMERICA

ISBN# 979-8-3507-2603-9

TABLE OF CONTENTS

There is no real agreement when it comes to defining what constitutes a *native plant*, but *Merriam-Webster* defines it like so:

> *native*: grown, produced, or originating in a particular place or in the vicinity: living or growing naturally in a particular region

For this book, we will stretch the definition to be "a plant that occurs naturally in the United States and is adapted to the Oklahoma climate." That means not all of the plants in this book are historically *native* to Oklahoma, although most are. It's worth noting that this definition might be perceived as more liberal than many accept, and we acknowledge and respect differing opinions on the matter. However, in the end, we decided to let gardeners decide for themselves.

We have also listed several *nativars*, or cultivars of native plants, that may have been selected for better flowering, color, size, or other growth characteristics.

The purpose of this book is to encourage the use of native plants in the ornamental landscape—for both what native plants can add visually to the landscape and also for the good they can do for the environment, and so we feel this liberal interpretation is appropriate.

INTRODUCTION

Anyone who believes gardening is easy does not live in the state of Oklahoma, where we have wind, cold, heat, wet, and dry—sometimes all in one week, sometimes all in a single day. Only plants that have evolved to handle such unpredictable, fluctuating weather conditions can flourish here.

Yet it is the norm, not the exception, to see homes and businesses landscaped without a single native plant. In fact, most Oklahoma landscapes are covered in plants from China, Japan, Europe, and Africa. Is it any wonder that such gardens suffer and become labor intensive?

These introduced plants provide little benefit to native wildlife, especially the birds, bees and butterflies, which are declining in frightening numbers due to the lack of food and habitat that native plants provide.

Why do Oklahomans not use more native plants in the garden? For one, people tend to plant what they know and what garden centers and seed catalogs promote. And two, many people believe that native plants only come in neutral tan and buff tones—which couldn't be further from the case.

We hope to dispel some of the myths and misconceptions about native plants with this book as we share the many reasons to use native plants, including:

- Their beauty, with flower and leaf colors that rival any plant outside of our borders.
- Their ability to evoke a sense of place, providing a reference to the native ecology.
- Their intrinsic value to enhance biodiversity, in stormwater management and erosion control.
- Their versatility, with plants as small as 4" to cover the ground up to those that grow hundreds of feet tall to provide shade and habitat.
- Their adaptability to the environment, as this is where they naturally evolved. Hence, the need for maintenance, irrigation, and chemical treatments is reduced.
- Their most important role in providing sustenance for native pollinator species such as birds, bees, and butterflies, all of which are declining in numbers and, in some cases, facing extinction. Can we live without these species? Not without a significant cost. These species eat our pests (mosquitoes and other unfavorable

7

insects) and provide beauty for our enjoyment. And, one out of every three bites of food that we eat depends on a pollinator to fertilize a plant.

Some believe that the next global crisis could arise due to depleting water resources. According to UNESCO (United Nations Educational, Scientific and Cultural Organization), "The global urban population facing water scarcity is projected to double to 1.7-2.4 billion people in 2050. The growing incidence of extreme and prolonged droughts is also stressing ecosystems, with dire consequences for both plant and animal species". To address this challenge, a shift in our approach to landscaping urban areas, parks, buildings, and residences is crucial. This means transitioning to plant species that thrive on the natural water supply available while simultaneously supporting local pollinators.

This book is written from the perspective of two licensed landscape architects, both of whom care about the way our landscape looks and functions ecologically. We hope to introduce municipalities, designers, and property owners to the joys and benefits of landscaping with native plants in a way that is beautiful and supports our natural environment.

Oklahoma is home to over 2,600 native plant species, each with its unique characteristics and uses. While not all of these species are considered ornamental or suitable for traditional landscaping, the selections featured in this book are both attractive and well-suited for Oklahoma.

This book does not aim to include all plants native to Oklahoma; instead, it focuses on those plants with which we have familiarity and hands-on experience and that work well as an ornamental plant. Our goal is to inspire you to incorporate these native plants into your own landscape.

This book is an update to our earlier publication, *Oklahoma Native Plants, a guide to designing landscapes to attract birds & butterflies*, published in 2019 (The Roadrunner Press). In response to the growing interest in native plants since then, we've expanded this edition to include more plants and additional advice on planting and maintaining native plants in Oklahoma. Groups like the Oklahoma Native Plant Society (https://oknativeplants.org) have become better known and the Oklahoma Native Plant Network (https://www.onpn.org/) was formed—both with goals to promote preservation and use of native plants.

This book shares the same format as the previous one, but with new recommendations. We hope that this update will encourage more people to plant native plants—to help support birds, bees, butterflies, improve soil ecosystems and for the enjoyment of people.

Growing a natural habitat garden is also one of the most important things each of us can do to help restore a little order to a disordered world.
- Ken Druse

To plant a garden is to dream of tomorrow
—Audrey Hepburn

HOW TO USE THIS BOOK

The plants in this book have been organized alphabetically by their botanical names per standard horticultural practice. You will also find the common name listed below it in the black bar. Additionally, we have included both a botanical name index and a common name index at the end of the book for cross-referencing.

Botanical / Scientific Names

Botanical, or scientific, names are distinctive and unchangeable labels assigned to individual plant species. They consist of Latin or Latinized terms and adhere to globally recognized standards, ensuring consistency.

These names serve as the universal language for scientists and professionals worldwide. Their adoption is crucial because common names can vary, subject to the preferences of growers or landscapers, and we want to ensure that you always purchase the plant you intended.

Once a genus of a plant is used on a page, the genus may be abbreviated, such as A. hubrichtii, instead of repeating the full name: Amsonia hubrichtii.

Common Names

Common names for plants may vary from country to country, state to state, and even from one nursery to another.

Common names can change as new people move to a region or old common names fall out of favor. In fact, some of the plants within this book are listed with more than one common name because their names can vary. In this book, the common names of plants will be capitalized.

Cultivar Names

Cultivars are simply variations of a plant species that have been selected for a certain trait. This might be flower color, size, foliage color, cold hardiness or other desired plant characteristic. For native plants, they are often referred to as 'nativars'. They may begin as chance seedlings found in the nursery or garden, or they may be deliberately bred for a special characteristic. Either way, the names of cultivars are designated with single quotation marks, for instance: Blond Ambition `Blue Grama' with 'Blue Grama' being the cultivar name, or Salvia greggi `Pink Preference', with `Pink Preference' being the cultivar name. The cultivar name helps the buyer know that a plant will produce the specific characteristics desired.

There is a lot of debate as to the value of nativars in their ability to attract and support pollinators. Many people would prefer that no nativars should be sold or planted. Some approve only of nativars that aren't significantly altered as far as bloom or leaf color, or the shape of flowers that might make it difficult for pollinators to reach. And others would plant any type of nativar regardless of their effect on the pollinators.

We understand and respect all sides of this discussion. As landscape architects, we understand the need for plants to be of a specific size or color to reflect the design intent, and so we will specify nativars when needed. Nativars are referenced in this book, with an explanation of their 'improved' traits. The reader can make their choice as to how they want to add to the landscape.

Description of Light Requirements

Full Sun: A location with more than six hours of sun per day.
Part Sun: A location that receives between four and six hours of sun per day or that receives dappled sun/shade all day.
Shade: A location that receives less than four hours of sun per day, with a preference to morning sun, rather than afternoon.

Top Twelve Plants for Monarchs

The "Top Twelve Plants for Monarchs" rankings are the work of Okies for Monarchs, a group that has identified plants that thrive in various parts of Oklahoma to support monarch butterflies. A summary of their recommendations of the "Top Twelve" is included in this book on page 104. For more information about their work, please visit: www.okiesformonarchs.org.

Native Plant Availability Description

Readily Available: Usually available wherever plants are sold.
Available from Good Nurseries: Available from professional landscape nurseries or garden centers.
Native Plant Growers: Usually available only from growers that specialize in growing and selling native plants.
Native Seed Growers: Available from seed producers who specialize in producing native seed. Local seed producers—those within two hundred miles of the planting site—are recommended for the best success.
Native Sod Producers: Available from some sod farms that specialize in providing native sod.

Pollinator Indicator

Provides food for butterflies and other insects

Provides food for birds

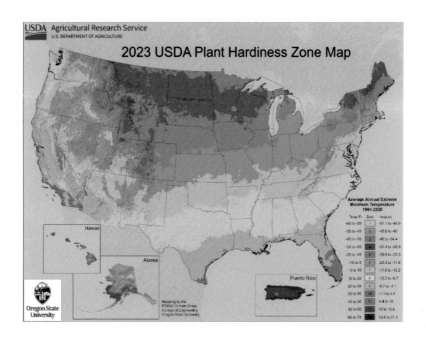

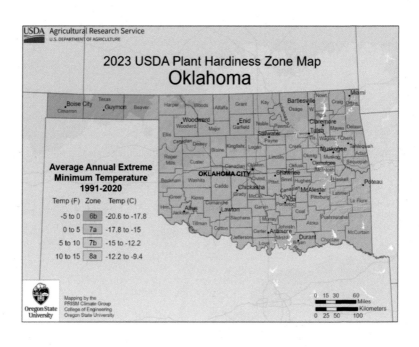

PLANT PROFILES: FORBS

Forbs are herbaceous flowering plants that are neither grasses nor woody species like shrubs or trees.

In this context, "forb" encompasses both annual and perennial plants typically cultivated for their attractive flower colors, leaf colors, and/or fragrances in landscaping.

Forbs play a critical role in providing sustenance for various wildlife, including birds, bees, butterflies, and other pollinators. Many forbs also offer significant nutritional value for small animals and livestock.

COMMON YARROW

Yarrow is one of the most controversial plants as to its origin—native, naturalized, or originally from Europe. I've seen all descriptions. With its fernlike leaves, it is frequently seen growing in Oklahoma meadows. The plant is extremely resistant to drought, especially when growing in the shade.

Common Yarrow can grow quite large—easily to 3' tall and can be somewhat aggressive in the ornamental garden. I have found yarrow growing naturally in a shady part of my backyard without any care. The plants slowly spread by underground rhizomes and can tolerate and flower in dry shade, making yarrow especially useful in the landscape.

There are nearly one hundred cultivars of yarrow in many colors including yellow, white, red, orange, and pink. The named cultivars tend to be much more compact, at 12-24" tall and thus easier to use in the landscape. Yarrow usually blooms in spring, but some plants will repeat bloom throughout the summer. Yarrow has a distinct sweet scent and is said to have many medicinal properties.

Readily Available
Size: 1-3 Feet Tall x 1-2 Feet Wide
Bloom: Many Colors / Normally Spring
Uses: Massing, Borders, Naturalizing, Ground Cover

USDA Zones: 3-9
Sun: Full Sun to Part Sun
Soil: Dry to Moist

NODDING ONION

Nodding Onion belongs to the allium family, which includes garlic, onions and chives. Like those plants, it is edible with a mild onion flavor.

The flowers are the most prominent feature: most often pale pink to purplish, and hanging gracefully from the stem, thus its name. Leaves are slender, grass-like up to 12" tall, and much like the other alliums they have a pungent smell when crushed.

Nodding Onion is naturally found in prairies, meadows and open woodlands, in well-drained sandy soils. Unlike other onions or chives, I have not had a problem with the plant spreading throughout the rest of my garden, although it is known to spread under more moist conditions.

Available from Native Plant Growers
Size: 1-2 Feet Tall x 1-Foot Wide
Bloom: Pink, Lavendar, White / Normally Spring
Uses: Naturalizing, Accent

USDA Zones: 3-9
Sun: Full Sun to Part Sun
Soil: Any

LEADPLANT

This is one tough plant! Leadplant needs absolutely no care at all and thrives in medium to dry soil. Leadplant takes a year or so to start to shine. I admit that I didn't think it was great when I first planted it. But after a few years, the foliage and the large purple flower spikes began to become showy. With its silvery gray foliage, leadplant can add interest to a bed, making it a great back-of-the-border or filler plant for locations that irrigation might not reach. Leadplant is a legume so it adds nitrogen back into the soil, which makes it an excellent companion plant for other species. Leadplant is extremely important to native bee populations.

Leadplant boasts a deep taproot, down to 20 feet! This makes it very drought tolerant and hard to transplant. Once mature, this plant might look better if cut back hard in spring to maintain a more compact shape.

Fragrant False Indigo, A. nana, is a close relative, but with green leaves and growth limited to about two feet.

Available from Native Plant Growers	**USDA Zones**: 2-9
Size: 2-3 Feet Tall x 2-3 Feet Wide	**Sun:** Full Sun to Part Sun
Bloom: Purple to Blue / July to August	**Soil:** Dry Sandy to Average
Uses: Naturalize, Erosion Control, Back of Border	

BLUESTAR

Bluestar is a well-behaved native plant that complements any ornamental or formal landscape design. Threadleaf Bluestar, A. hubrichtii, provides beautiful, delicate, fine-textured leaves that can reach heights of 3 feet or more.

Blue Star, A. tabernaemontana, is actually a better plant for pollinators. It offers similar flowers and growth habits, but it has larger leaves and tends to be a shorter plant topping out at 20 inches in height. The cultivar 'Blue Ice' is more compact at 12-15" tall.

Both plants have intense, pale blue, star-shaped flowers early in spring. However, it is in fall when they really shine. Bluestar's vivid, breathtaking yellow-gold fall color adds an outstanding splash of color to any landscape. The plant performs best with regular irrigation and in lower pH soils.

Both of these plants are easy to grow with few pests and deer tend to avoid them.

Available from Good Nurseries
Size: 2-3 Feet Tall x 2-3 Feet Wide
Bloom: Pale Blue /April to May
Uses: Massing, Mid Border, Accent, Rain Garden

USDA Zones: 5-8
Sun: Full Sun to Part Sun
Soil: Moist, Rich Garden Soil

PRAIRIE PUSSYTOES

CREDIT: NATIVE PLANTS NURSERY

What a fun plant! This is a great groundcover for dry, shady areas with silvery-green, velvety leaves, which is what the plant is known for. In late spring, the flowers stand up about a foot and look like little cat's paws, thus the name. Pussytoes can go partially of dormant in the heat of summer, but quickly recovers once the days get shorter, spreading by stolons. This makes a great groundcover and container plant. Can be added as a green filler between other plants.

This is a plant best suited to dry, rocky lean soils-not clay. Parts of the plant are poisonous so deer and rabbits and other small animals won't touch them.

Available from Good Nurseries
Size: 8 Inches Tall
Bloom: White /April to May
Uses: Naturalize, Groundcover

USDA Zones: 3-8
Sun: Full Sun to Part Shade
Soil: medium to well-drained soils
Poisonous Plant Parts

Aquilegia canadensis

COLUMBINE

Even though Columbine will technically grow in sunny locations; in Oklahoma, it is best to grow it in the shade. Ideal conditions include rich, well-drained or moist garden soil where it will flower in many colors. When temperatures reach 90 degrees or higher, the plant may go dormant, or even die, unless it is watered well and protected from sun and wind.

A delicate-looking plant with beautiful flowers and small fern-like leaves, Columbine's blooms can be extended significantly with regular deadheading. Texas Gold Columbine, A. chrysantha var hinckleyana, is better adapted to the Oklahoma heat and has a bright yellow flower.

Columbine is a short-lived perennial, but it will re-seed and spread readily. Also, the flowers attract hummingbirds.

Available from Good Nurseries
Size: 1-3 Feet Tall x 1-3 Feet Wide
Bloom: Red, Yellow, Pink, Blue/March to April
Uses: Woodland, Shady Border, Ground Cover

USDA Zones: 3-8
Sun: Part Sun to Shade
Soil: Rich, Well Drained, Moist Garden Soil

If you love monarch butterflies, you must plant milkweed. The plants are vital for the monarch butterfly's life cycle, serving as the exclusive host during the butterfly's larval phase. In other words, the Monarch caterpillar will only eat Milkweed leaves; without them, there will be no Monarchs.

There are seventy-three species of native milkweed in this country, with at least twenty that are native to Oklahoma. Of those, one can be found for every type of soil, size, or bloom time—although they all prefer a sunny location. Several of these species are described on the following pages. Additional information can be found on the Okies for Monarchs website (okiesformonarhcs.org).

Ideally, Milkweed should be planted in groups of at least two species with as many as ten plants in an area that would bloom at different times.

You will find that most Milkweeds will have aphids at some point. They are not a problem unless the plant shows stress. If so, spray the plant and aphids with soapy water or just ahigh-pressure water hose. Do NOT spray insecticide of any type of the milkweed as it will kill the caterpillars or monarchs that we want to save.

SWAMP MILKWEED

The Swamp Milkweed is one of the most important food sources for the monarch. I've seen this plant covered in caterpillars even while a neighboring Butterfly Weed (A. tuberosa) remains untouched. The fragrant flowers are bright and showy on top of a tall branching stem. These flowers attract native bees and provide nectar to butterflies and hummingbirds. The seedpods are also showy, similar to other milkweeds.

True to its name, Swamp Milkweed thrives in consistently wet and marshy environments, along edges of ponds and streams and in heavy, moist, clay, and mucky soils. It prefers sun but can tolerate some shade.

Swamp Milkweed is slow to emerge from dormancy in spring, so it is nice to mark a new plant's location. My experience is that it also does not come back every year—or maybe I didn't wait long enough? Or, maybe (likely) I didn't give it the irrigation that it needs.

Available from Native Plant Growers
Poisonous; all plant parts may irritate skin or cause illness

Size: 3-4 Feet Tall and wide
Bloom: Pink-Mauve or white / June-Oct.
Uses: Wetland Gardens

USDA Zones: 4-9
Sun: Full Sun- Part Shade
Soil: Prefers Moist

COMMON MILKWEED

Common Milkweed is tall, with purplish blooms, and thrives in moist soil conditions. The plant is fragrant when blooming and will spread by rhizomes and self-seed year after year. It can be aggressive in garden soils and it is best located at the edge of a field, and not in the garden.

Common milkweed is like the Walmart for insects—with something for everyone. Over 450 insects will feed on some portion of the plant, whether flowers, sap, or leaves. It is one of the most important plants for the monarch caterpillar.

Available from Native Plant Growers
Poisonous; all plant parts may irritate skin or cause illness
Size: 5 Feet Tall x 5 Feet Wide, spreading   **USDA Zones:** 4-9
Bloom: White, Purple / August to October   **Sun:** Full Sun
Uses: Mid-Back Border, Naturalizing   **Soil:** Moist

BUTTERFLY WEED

Butterfly Weed is the plant we usually think of when planting for monarchs. A compact plant with bright fiery-orange flowers that appear off and on throughout the summer, the plant is super easy to grow and striking when in bloom. Just remember that Butterfly Weed breaks dormancy later than most other plants in spring so don't give up on it!

When the plant starts putting out seed, it can be a little messy, but that stage is easily hidden if you plant it among other low plants. Some people say that Butterfly Weed will spread and reseed. I haven't found this to be a problem, and wouldn't mind if it did a little. Butterfly Weed does not transplant easily because of its deep tap root.

While butterfly weed is good for monarchs, it doesn't seem to be their favorite. In my experience, they prefer other Asclepias species, if available. The plant is listed as one of the top twelve plants for monarchs, and it is resistant to deer.

Available from Good Nurseries

Poisonous; all plant parts may irritate skin or cause illness

Size: 1-2 Feet Tall x 1 Foot Wide   **USDA Zones:** 3-9

Bloom: Yellow, Orange / May to September   **Sun:** Full Sun

Uses: Naturalize, Borders, Massing   **Soil:** Dry to Medium, Well-Drained

WHORLED MILKWEED

CREDIT: NATIVE PLANTS NURSERY

CREDIT: NATIVE PLANTS NURSERY

After much study, I believe this is the Milkweed for my garden. It is one of the monarch's favorites, it's beautiful and it likes dry habitats. Since I don't irrigate much, this is perfect. Whorled Milkweed is not as aggressive as the common Milkweed and it is shorter, only growing to about 2' tall. It has white flowers in late spring to early summer and delicate, narrow, leaves whorled along the stem.

Whorled Milkweed is commonly seen along Oklahoma ditches and road banks with well-drained soil, making it a hardy and attractive addition to the garden.

Available from Native Plant Growers
Poisonous; all plant parts may irritate skin or cause illness
Size: 1-3 Feet Tall and wide   **USDA Zones:** 3-9
Bloom: Pale pink to white / May-September   **Sun:** Full Sun- Part Shade
Uses: Borders, Meadow Gardens, Naturalize   **Soil:** Prefers Dry, rocky, sandy

Asclepias viridis

Because Green Milkweed blooms earlier than other milkweeds, experts consider it one of the most important milkweeds when it comes to supporting monarch butterflies. The plant attracts monarchs on their spring migration through Oklahoma.

Green Milkweed has subtle purplish-white flowers and large seeds, making it less flashy than some other milkweeds. However, its upright growth habit makes it a great filler plant for borders or naturalizing. It thrives in poor, rocky, and dry soils.

A similar species, A. asperula (Antelope-Horns) is more common in the dry western part of the state and is highly valuable to butterflies. This plant is listed as one of the top twelve plants for monarchs.

Available from Native Plant Growers
Poisonous; Sap May Irritate Skin
Size: 1-2 Feet Tall x 1-2 Feet Wide   **USDA Zones**: 3-9
Bloom: White, green, purple/ April to September   **Sun**: Full Sun
Uses: Naturalize, Borders   **Soil**: Rich or Poor Soil

BLUE FALSE INDIGO

Blue False Indigo is a lovely, early-spring blooming plant showcasing foot-long spikes of blue, pealike flowers during May and June. After flowering, the large, gray seedpods remain interesting for the rest of the year.

The plant grows best in dry to medium soils, although it can tolerate drought and poor soils. Plants grow in expanding clumps of blue-green foliage in a shrub-like habit. The plant has a deep taproot, helping to make it drought tolerant and easy to grow and hard to transplant. Trimming foliage after blooming will help maintain a neat plant appearance, if the seedpods aren't desired.

Yellow Wild Indigo, B. sphaerocarpa, is a similar, compact plant that is equally striking with bright yellow blooms.

Baptista is classified in the pea family and, as with other legumes, has a symbiotic relationship with soil-dwelling bacteria that makes it capable of fixing nitrogen in the soil.

Available from Native Plant Growers	**USDA Zones:** 3-8
Size: 3-4 Feet Tall x 3-4 Feet Wide	**Sun:** Full Sun to Part Sun
Bloom: Indigo Blue / May to June	**Soil:** Dry to Medium
Uses: Borders, Meadow Gardens, Naturalize	

CHOCOLATE DAISY, CHOCOLATE FLOWER

The scent of Chocolate Daisy is incredibly fragrant, reminiscent of rich chocolate cake, especially in the morning. Even better, this plant has a profusion of yellow flowers that bloom nearly all summer. It is tolerant of drought, heat, dry rocky and sandy soils and will grow in sun or part shade. This is a very low maintenance plant, but it does not handle heavy wet soils.

Chocolate Daisy will re-seed, but not to excess, making it perfect for sharing with friends. You can collect seeds in summer and then plant the following spring or just transplant the seedlings from near the mother plant in the spring. This would be a fun plant to add to any children's or sensory garden.

Makes a nice cut flower. You can mow the plants after the first flowering in a wildflower planting. It is also deer resistant.

Available from Native Plant Growers
Size: 1-3 Feet Tall x 2 Feet Wide
Bloom: Yellow / April to November
Uses: Borders, Meadow Gardens, Naturalize

USDA Zones: 3-8
Sun: Full Sun to Part Sun
Soil: Dry to Medium

PURPLE POPPY MALLOW, WINECUP

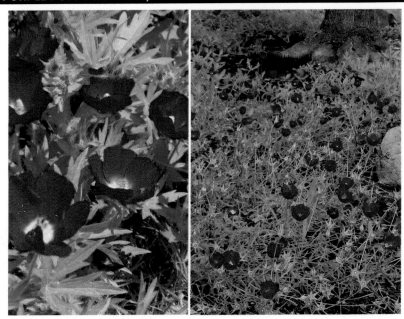

Poppy Mallow is a common, spring-blooming wildflower often seen growing naturally along Oklahoma roads, with its abundant purplish-red flowers. This low-growing, sprawling ground-cover plant is not only tough but also low-maintenance. It can be used in a variety of locations, and looks great trailing over walls or mixed with other low-growing perennials. Try pairing Poppy Mallow with Butterfly weed (A. tuberosa) or other plants that bloom later in the season, because when temperatures get too hot, Poppy Mallow may go dormant and this will allow your summer bloomers to take over.

Poppy Mallow has a deep tuberous taproot, which makes it drought tolerant. If irrigated well, the plant will bloom all summer.

Tall Poppy Mallow, (C. leiocarpa) has very similar flowers, but grows taller, as high as 3' tall. It is an annual that will reseed freely in sandy, well-drained soils and full sun.

Available from Native Plant Growers
Size: 6-12 Inches Tall x 3 Feet Wide
Bloom: Magenta /April to May
Uses: Ground Cover, Rock Garden, Border Front

USDA Zones: 3-8
Sun: Full Sun to Part Sun
Soil: Sandy, Loam, Clay

Conoclinium coelestinum

BLUE MISTFLOWER

Blue Mistflower attracts both bees and butterflies. In my back yard, I have witnessed as many as a dozen monarch butterflies at a single time covering my small four-square-foot patch of Blue Mistflower plants. During the fall migration, butterflies stop and feast on the nectar of the many blue flowers. This plant is also called Wild Ageratum, due to the similarity of the fluffy blue flowers to the annual plant.

Blue Mistflower boasts a bluish-violet bloom that protrudes approximately a foot above the foliage. This plant tolerates both shady and sunny locations, but I find its value to be in the shade where we always need more flowering plants.

This plant spreads through underground roots but is well-behaved in shady locations. It can be somewhat aggressive in sunny areas but is easily pulled up.

Available from Native Plant Growers
Size: 1-3 Feet Tall x 1 Foot Wide
Bloom: Blue, Purple / July to November
Uses: Ground Cover, Shade Garden

USDA Zones: 5-10
Sun: Full Sun to Shade
Soil: Any

Coreopsis lanceolata

LANCELEAF COREOPSIS

When I moved into my home, I discovered small, yellow-blooming plants pop up each spring and quickly cover any free space in my new garden. Initially, I'd remove them after flowering, but now I leave these prolific bloomers in place as ground cover among my perennials and grasses. Coreopsis spreads but is easily controlled.

The plant blooms for several weeks each spring with two- to three-inch-long yellow rays of petals encircling a greenish-yellow disk. Deadheading extends the bloom time significantly. Loved by bees, butterflies, and people, Coreopsis is a perennial that reseeds naturally, and is often found along Oklahoma roadways. It is low-maintenance, evergreen and very easy to grow.

Available from Good Nurseries	**USDA Zones:** 4-9
Size: 1-2 Feet Tall x 1-2 Feet Wide	**Sun**: Full Sun to Part Sun
Bloom: Yellow / May to July	**Soil**: Any
Uses: Ground Cover, Massing, Naturalizing	

PLAINS COREOPSIS, Golden Tickseed

      Plains Coreopsis is an annual plant, yet its self-seeding nature ensures a consistent presence in your garden. It is the most common wildflower in Oklahoma, frequently seen in moist ditches, along roadsides, cultivated fields and wildflower meadows in wet seasons. Its distinctive yellow and red blossoms, perched atop slender stems, make it easily recognizable and a magnet for birds and butterflies.

      Sow seeds in late fall or early spring for easy germination. Plains Coreopsis is deer resistant and is relatively pest free.

Available from Native Seed Suppliers
Size: 2-4 Feet Tall x 1-2 Feet Wide
Bloom: Red, Yellow, Brown / June to September
Uses: Naturalizing, Wildflower meadows

USDA Zones: 2-11
Sun: Full Sun to Part Shade
Soil: Prefers moist, sandy

Tall Coreopsis lives up to its name, soaring to six feet or more in a partial sun area of my garden. It starts blooming just as Large Coneflower, (R. maxima), finishes. That makes them great companion plants, extending the yellow bloom period and structurally supporting each other's tall foliage. Butterflies love the flowers, while the seeds become a feast for birds, so don't be in a rush to trim those seed heads. I usually wait until the following spring.

Division of the plant every two to three years is recommended, but I haven't found it necessary in the four years I have enjoyed this beautiful, low-maintenance, and durable plant. Coreopsis is very tolerant of heat, humidity, and drought.

Available from Native Plant Growers
Size: 3-6 Feet Tall x 2-3 Feet Wide
Bloom: Yellow, Orange / July to September
Uses: Accent, Massing, Rock Gardens

USDA Zones: 3-8
Sun: Full Sun to Part Sun
Soil: Dry to Medium

Coreopsis verticillata

THREADLEAF COREOPSIS

Threadleaf Coreopsis are low-growing, compact plants with threadlike dark green leaves and tiny flowers, offering an elegant, airy appearance. Don't let their dainty form fool you, as they are tough bloomers and give back to birds and butterflies. The plants have an extended bloom period and spread by rhizomes. Like other Coreopsis, they are tolerant of heat, humidity, and drought.

There are many cultivars of this native tickseed with different names and colors, including 'Tweety', 'Moonbeam' , and 'Pink', among others.

Pruning plants mid-year will promote a second flush of blooms in the fall. Plants respond well to being divided every three to four years to increase vigor, while giving you additional plants.

Readily Available   **USDA Zones**: 3-9
Size: 1-3 Feet Tall x 2 Feet Wide   **Sun**: Full Sun-Partial Shade
Bloom: Yellow, Orange, Pink / July to September   **Soil**: Dry to Medium
Uses: Accent, Borders, Massing, Rock Gardens

PURPLE PRAIRIE CLOVER

Purple Prairie Clover is an easily grown, low-maintenance plant with striking purple/rose flowers. Its fine texture and tiny purple flowers, flecked with gold on a cone-like flower head, create a unique look. The flowers have a distinct blooming pattern, starting at the base of the head and gradually moves upward throughout the season, lasting approximately one month.

This plant has a deep taproot which makes it very drought tolerant. Naturally found in rocky, well-drained prairies, it's less suited to heavy clay soils.

Purple Prairie Clover benefits a variety of butterflies and bees by offering nectar and pollen, and under favorable conditions, it may self-seed. For an interesting mix, pair this plant with White Prairie Clover (D. candida) due to their similar growth habits.

As a nitrogen-fixing legume, it serves as a valuable companion in the garden, naturally enriching the soil and enhancing the growth of other plants.

Available from Native Plant Growers	**USDA Zones**: 3-8
Size: 1-3 Feet Tall x 1-2 Feet Wide	**Sun**: Full Sun
Bloom: Rose/Purple / June to August	**Soil**: Average, Well-Drained
Uses: Border, Massing, Naturalize	

Echinacea pallida
PALE PURPLE CONEFLOWER

Pale Purple Coneflower resembles Purple Coneflower, with very pale purple to pink flowers but with much thinner petals. Blooming earlier than its counterpart, these two complement each other, creating an extended bloom period.

Pale Purple Coneflower is a long-lived perennial with a deep tap root, and is very drought tolerant, once established.

This plant looks great in a grassland planting.

Available from Native Plant Growers
Size: 2-3 Feet Tall x 1-2 Feet Wide
Bloom: Pink / June to July
Uses: Accent, Border, Ground Cover, Naturalize

USDA Zones: 3-8
Sun: Full Sun to Partial Shade
Soil: Medium-Well Drained

Echinacea purpurea

PURPLE CONEFLOWER

Purple Coneflower has a distinct flower - with a large, rust-colored conical disk in the center topping colorful, drooping petals. Even after the petals drop, the centers stay until the seeds ripen, ensuring year-round interest.

A fantastic full-sun plant, the Coneflower also tolerates and flowers in partial shade. Its diverse height range makes it a good option for borders as well as large meadow plantings. The plant grows so easily; just sow seeds directly into the garden in early spring or late fall.

There are many different cultivars of Coneflower with an array of flower colors ranging from white to purple in sizes that range from two to five feet. But, be wary of those cultivars that have been so changed from the original that the benefits to pollinators may be compromised.

Recognized among the top twelve plants for monarchs, Coneflower attracts birds, bees, and other pollinators. It is also a deer resistant plant.

Available from Good Nurseries	**USDA Zones:** 3-8
Size: 2-5 Feet Tall x 1-2 Feet Wide	**Sun:** Full Sun to Shade
Bloom: White, Purple, Pink / June to August	**Soil:** Any
Uses: Accent, Border, Ground Cover, Naturalize	

ENGELMANN'S DAISY, CUTLEAF DAISY

Engelmann's Daisy is one of the most adaptable plants native to Oklahoma, thriving in almost any soil condition and in all but the deepest shade. I attest to its durability and low-maintenance nature, as I planted this beautiful plant at my father's house and—despite his <u>never</u> watering it—the plant continued to thrive.

Bursting with bright yellow daisies from spring through the fall, this well-behaved plant maintains a nice, compact 2-foot height. It will reseed, but, even the smallest seedlings have such a deep tap root, it is hard to get a good transplant.

This is one of my favorite plants because of its long bloom period— it has a place in everyone's garden.

Deadheading the flowers prolongs the blooming season. While livestock find it delicious, Engelmann's Daisy is resistant to deer and rabbits, making it a hardy choice for all landscapes.

Available from Native Plant Growers
Size: 1-3 Feet Tall x 1-2 Feet Wide
Bloom: Yellow / April to August
Uses: Accent, Mid-Back Border, Naturalize

USDA Zones: 5-10
Sun: Full Sun to Part Sun
Soil: Any

Equisetum hyemale

HORSETAIL

While beautiful and interesting when growing in its native habitat, Equisetum, or horsetail, is not usually appropriate for the ornamental landscape. Unless restricted with a concrete barrier, it quickly spreads into lawns and other planting areas, proving extremely difficult to eradicate, similar to bamboo. BE VERY CAREFUL! It is important to know that any section containing nodes from its stem or rhizome can sprout a new plant, increasing its capacity to become invasive.

This plant is known for its strict hollow stems with jointed segments accented by slender black bands, this evergreen lacks flowers and has minimal appeal to pollinators.

Adaptable to various soils, it thrives in medium to wet conditions and can even tolerate standing water.

In water gardens, contain the plant in pots to restrict both height and spread.

Available from Good Nurseries	**USDA Zones:** 4-9
Size: 2-4 Feet Tall x 1-6 Feet Spread	**Sun:** Full Sun
Bloom: None	**Soil:** Prefers Wet, Tolerates Any
Uses: Accent, Water Gardens	

Eryngium yuccifolium

RATTLESNAKE MASTER

Rattlesnake Master has such an unusual flower one might think its common name stems from its spiky bloom—but no. One of the most reliable stories suggest that native peoples would use the dried flower heads as ceremonial rattles.

This unique plant is a standout, sure to catch the eye and spark curiosity among your neighbors. The plant's large, sword-shaped leaves resemble those of the yucca and the thistle-like flower heads attract a wide array of small native bees, soldier beetles, butterflies, wasps, and flies.

The thick hollow stems double as nesting sites for tunnel-nesting bees. Thanks to its taproot, this plant is very drought tolerant. The plant has a tendency to flop over, so site it with other tall plants that can support it. I have planted mine in wire cages to help them stay upright.

The flower makes an interesting cut flower in arrangements. A member of the carrot family, it ranks among one of the top twelve plants for monarchs.

Available from Native Plant Growers   **USDA Zones:** 3-8
Size: 4-5 Feet Tall x 2-3 Feet Wide   **Sun:** Full Sun
Bloom: Greenish White / June to September   **Soil:** Prefers Dry, Tolerant any
Uses: Accent, Naturalize, Meadow

SNOW ON THE MOUNTAIN

The most striking feature of Snow on the Mountain is its variegated foliage. The leaves are green, with white, pink or light green margins, which give the plant its name. When flowering, the inconspicuous flowers are surrounded by showy bracts, similar to poinsettias, but in shades of pink or white, creating an attractive contrast with the foliage.

This plant normally reaches from 1 to 3' tall and is easily grown from seeds directly sown in the garden in spring after the last frost. It can self-seed easily and naturalize. The plant is drought tolerant, and grows best in xeriscape and naturalized areas. It is frequently seen growing in fields or on roadsides.

Available from Native Seed Producers Poisonous: can be toxic if ingested; sap may be irritating to the skin and eyes. **USDA Zones:** 2-11

Size: 1-3 Feet Tall x 1-2 Feet Wide   **Sun**: Full Sun

Bloom: Greenish-yellow/July to September   **Soil**: Dry to Medium, well-drained, tolerant of rocky soils

Uses: Accent, Naturalize, Borders, Rock Gardens

SWEET JOE PYE WEED

The unique common names of plants have always intrigued me, but it took several years to locate the fragrant Joe Pye Weed, which is named after a Native American herbalist. This wildflower can reach eight feet high in Oklahoma and adds texture to a garden, while creating a colorful backdrop for small plants. Joe Pye Weed has tiny, pinkish purple flowers in large compound blooms attracting Monarchs, Swallowtails and many other butterflies. The leaves and flowers give off a vanilla scent when crushed. To maintain a shorter and sturdier plant, consider cutting it back before July 1st, allowing for flowering in August.

Baby Joe Pye, (E. dubium 'Baby Joe'), is a dwarf version of the plant, topping out at just two or three feet. Both plants prefer some irrigation to perform best. They are ideally sited near the edge of a stream or pond to ensure enough moisture.

Available from Native Plant Growers
Size: 5-8 Feet Tall x 3-4 Feet Wide
Bloom: White, Pink, Purple / July to September
Uses: Massing, Naturalize, Rain or Woodland Garden

USDA Zones: 4-9
Sun: Full Sun to Shade
Soil: Wet to Medium-Wet, Tolerates Clay

WILD STRAWBERRY

Wild Strawberry makes a nice, low-growing ground cover. I had a large patch of Wild Strawberry growing on the north side of my house when I moved in. At the time I found it too aggressive, and I removed it, which was a big mistake. Apparently, Wild Strawberry is that rare plant that loves shade and lousy clay soil.

This neat plant looks just like the strawberry plant you plant for fruit, but with smaller leaves and fruit. Wild Strawberry produces small, white flowers followed by small, tart, edible berries in summer. The value of this plant is as a ground cover thick enough to choke out weeds and still maintain its beauty. Wild Strawberry can become aggressive and overtake desired plants, so plant it where it can spread. This can be a nice alternative to lawn, tolerating foot traffic well.

As a member of the rose family Wild Strawberry attracts birds, butterflies, and wildlife, and it can tolerate deer, drought, erosion, and mildly acidic soil.

Available from Native Plant Growers	**USDA Zones:** 5-9
Size: 4-8 Inches Tall	**Sun:** Full Sun to Shade
Bloom: White / April to June	**Soil:** Any
Uses: Spreading Ground Cover	

Gaillardia aristata

COMMON BLANKETFLOWER

The Common Blanketflower typically grows in clumps up to 30" tall on dry meadows, prairies, and grasslands. The showy flower blooms from late spring to fall and are attractive to butterflies, while Goldfinches are attracted to the seeds in the fall. The reference to "blanket flower" is likely due to the resemblance of the warm flower colors to blankets woven by Native Americans.

Root rot may occur in wet soils and powdery mildew may occur during wet seasons.

Available from Native Plant Growers
Size: 10-12 Inches tall and wide
Bloom: Orange/Red / May to September
Uses: Borders, rock gardens, container gardening

USDA Zones: 3-8
Sun: Full Sun
Soil: Dry

Gaillardia pulchella   *ANNUAL*

INDIAN BLANKET

The state wildflower of Oklahoma since 1986, Indian Blanket adds bold, fiery color into the summer gardens or meadows. A tough and extremely showy member of the daisy family, the plant includes many cultivars with double flowering and color options.

This annual plant also called Firewheel, it is easily grown in full sun and sandy, rocky soils. If grown in rich soils, the plant will become taller and, flop over.

Sow the seeds directly into the garden either in the fall or after the last spring frost. Prolong the bloom period by deadheading, but be sure to leave some spent flowerheads for the birds to eat and to supply next year's plants. Indian Blanket will reseed in optimal conditions. A beautiful cut flower, this plant is loved by native bees and butterflies.

Available: Native Seed Producers, Native Plant Growers **USDA** Zones: 2-10
Size: 1-2 feet Tall   **Sun**: Full Sun
Bloom: Red Center, Yellow Fringe / May to August   **Soil**: Dry to Medium
Uses: Annuals, Naturalizing, Borders, Rock Gardens

ROSE VERBENA, ROSE VERVAIN

Rose Verbena is an easily grown, low-spreading, perennial ground cover with pink flowers and hairy stems that take root when they touch with the ground.

It grows thick enough to choke out weeds. Its attractive, long-blooming flowers has led to the introduction of several cultivars, expanding the color palette beyond typical native plants.

'Homestead' is a pretty spectacular cultivar, with show-stopping blooms all year long in exquisite deep purple, red, or pink. Purple is by far my favorite as shown above left. It blends nicely with other blue and white bloomers and contrasts nicely with yellow and orange ones.

A common, easily found ornamental plant that should be used more often. I have never had any insect problems with it, although occasionally it will suffer some winter damage with a partial die-off.

Verbena is deer resistant, but attracts birds and butterflies.

Readily Available
Size: 6-12 Inches Tall x 18-24 Inches Wide
Bloom: Purple, Red, Pink, White / May to October
Uses: Containers, Ground Cover, Massing, Rock Gardens

USDA Zones: 5-9
Sun: Full Sun
Soil: Dry to Medium
Well-Drained

Helianthus augustifolius

NARROW-LEAF SUNFLOWER, SWAMP SUNFLOWER

I got this plant as an experiment and wow, did it impress! This plant started out innocently enough, but soon surpassed my height. Before the summer's end, it surprised me with spectacular 2-inch yellow flowers with narrow petals covering the plant.

While the name implies that it needed a lot of water, this plant did fine in my garden without any additional irrigation. It is large and can easily get 7' tall by 3' wide, so give it a lot of space. It is a back-of the border or accent plant.

This plant attracts tons of pollinators, bees, butterflies and birds. It is a joy to witness.

Available from Native Plant Growers
Size: 5-8 Feet Tall x 3 Feet Wide
Bloom: Gold-Yellow/September to Frost
Uses: Accent, Back Border, Mass Plantings

USDA Zones: 3-8
Sun: Full Sun to Part Sun
Soil: Any, will take wet or swampy soils

MAXIMILIAN SUNFLOWER, PRAIRIE SUNFLOWER

This is the sunflower that you see on the sides of country roads and in open fields in the fall. In those drought-plagued locations, it can grow to four feet tall with beautiful yellow flowers. Under more favorable growing conditions, Maximilian Sunflower can reach ten feet in height! It has large 2-3" flowers starting in late summer and extending into the fall, reaching its fullest potential in moist ditches in full sun. A native prairie perennial, it produces a heavy seed crop, providing needed forage for livestock, goldfinches, and other wildlife.

The plant can be messy at the base so it is best planted in the back of the border or behind lower grasses. If planted in overly fertile soil the plants may need to be staked prior to flowering. It spreads from rhizomes and reseeding.

A fun fact: The plant's unique structure makes it a challenge for squirrels to climb, ensuring that birds, not squirrels, typically enjoy the seeds.

Available from Native Plant Growers   **USDA Zones**: 3-8
Size: 6-10 Feet Tall x 3 Feet Wide   **Sun**: Full Sun to Part Sun
Bloom: Yellow, with Orange Center/August to October **Soil**: Any
Uses: Accent, Back Border, Mass Plantings

Heliopsis helianthoides

FALSE SUNFLOWER, OX-EYE DAISY

False Sunflower provides a long, summer bloom, making it an excellent addition to naturalized areas or prairie settings. This perennial is remarkably easy to grow with drought-tolerant characteristics, and attractive sunflower-like flowers, with orange-yellow rays shooting out from brown center disks.

If grown in partial shade or nutrient rich soils, the plant may need staking in order to stay upright. Alternately, the stems can be cut back by one-third to one-half in May to reduce the height of the plant. If left at its full height, False Sunflower is great as a cut flower. No matter its height, the plant will attract butterflies and hummingbirds.

Available from Native Plant Growers
Size: 3-6 Feet Tall x 2-4 Feet Wide
Bloom: Orange-Yellow, Brown Center / June to August
Uses: Back Border, Cut Flower, Naturalized

USDA Zones: 3-9
Sun: Full Sun
Soil: Any

HEUCHERA, CORAL BELLS, ALUMNROOT

Heuchera, also known as Coral Bells, is an evergreen perennial wildflower with a mounding growth habit, thriving in shaded to partially sunny, moist woodlands.

While its flower displays are not often showy, it does provide a light texture to the landscape. Cultivars display colorful evergreen leaves that remind me of the annual Coleus plant. The foliage comes in red, purple, lime, peach, green, or silvery green and makes a striking statement even without flowers. However, the cultivars seem to possess less vigor.

The pink, red, or white flower clusters at the end of tall, wiry stalks can extend fifteen inches above the base of the plant. Despite being natives and nativars, Heuchera requires a higher level of maintenance, including protection from the sun, good air circulation to prevent diseases, winter mulching, rich soils, and perfect drainage.

Readily Available
Size: 1-2 Feet Tall x 1-2 Feet Wide
Bloom: Greenish-White / June to August
Uses: Ground Cover, Rock Garden, Raised Beds

USDA Zones: 4-9
Sun: Full to part shade
Soil: Organically Rich, Moist, Well Drained

It doesn't seem like Hardy Hibiscus, or Rose Mallow would be native to Oklahoma and truthfully, it is best planted in very wet areas, along streams, or in places with regular irrigation. But, we have those in Oklahoma, too! This plant produces beautiful 6-inch diameter flowers on equally large three-lobed leaves, it's often called Halberd-leaf Rose Mallow due to the shape of its arrowhead or spear-shaped leaves.

This is a stunning plant that will grow well in full sun as long as its high-water needs are met. The large flowers attract bees, butterflies and hummingbirds. Seeds are a food source for various birds.

Readily Available
Size: 4-6 Feet Tall x 2-3 Feet Wide
Bloom: White-Pink with maroon eyes/
August-September

USDA Zones: 4-9
Sun: Full Sun
Soil: Organically Rich, medium-wet

Uses: Near water or low spots, back of border, cottage garden, wetland

DENSE GAYFEATHER

The Liatris, or Gayfeathers are showy native plants with flowers that look like purple exclamation marks; lasting from late summer through early fall. Similar to other fall-blooming plants, they are like candy to monarchs on their fall migration and is listed as one of the top twelve plants for monarchs.

The plant is easy to grow and can be a long-lasting addition to the garden as long as soil is well-drained. It looks and performs best when planted in groups of three or more. Liatris may be grown from seed, but it is slow to establish.

Dense Gayfeather, L spicata is two to six feet tall that prefers moist soils. Both Tall Gayfeather, L. Aspera (two to three feet tall) and Praire Blazingstar, L. Pycnostrachya (two to five feet tall) will prefer poor, dry sandy soils.

`Kobold' is a lower-growing cultivar that tops out at about two-feet tall, and so does not need staking.

Available from Good Nurseries   **USDA Zones:** 3-9
Size: 2-5 Feet Tall x 1-2 Feet Wide   **Sun:** Full Sun to Part Sun
Bloom: Rose, Purple or White / August to October   **Soil:** Well-Drained
Uses: Accent, Border, Cut Flowers, Massing, Rock Garden

Lobelia cardinalis
CARDINAL FLOWER

Gardens occasionally have a place that is wet and swampy or with poor drainage where nothing grows. That spot is ideal for Cardinal Flower, which may be the perfect water garden plant. It must be sited carefully, along streams, ponds, springs, and in low, damp, wooded areas. Soil around Cardinal plants should be kept moist at all times and the plant will even tolerate flooding for brief periods.

The showy, eight-inch-long flower spikes feature bright red terminal flowers that attract hummingbirds which are necessary for pollinating this plant in late summer and early fall.

This plant is best grown where it gets morning sun and afternoon shade, it also benefits from mulching to help hold in moisture. The short-lived perennial can be propagated by bending and fastening a stem into the mud.

Available from Native Plant Growers: All plant parts are toxic if swallowed.
Size: 2-4 Feet Tall x 1-2 Feet Wide
Bloom: Red / July to September
Uses: Naturalize, Near Ponds/Streams,

USDA Zones: 3-9
Sun: Full Sun to Part Sun
Soil: Moist, Water Garden

TURK'S CAP

CREDIT: LAURIE EFFINGER

True red flowers are unusual to find in nature but Turk's Cap, also known as Ladies's Eardrops, Scotchman's Purse, and Wild Fuchsia, has them. The blooms are small but numerous, with swirled petals that always look about to open but never do. The flowers' bright red color is very showy and attractive. The plant's deep green leaves span up to five inches, making for a stark contrast to the smaller flowers. Turk's Cap blooms through the summer heat and into the cool of fall, with mounded foliage that attracts butterflies, bees, and hummingbirds.

Turk's Cap usually freezes back to the ground during harsh winters. When this happens, cut back and remove all dead materials in the following spring to allow new shoots to emerge. Even without a freeze, it is still a good idea to cut the plant back to encourage new growth. The plant can be late to emerge from dormancy, but it is worth the wait. This plant is resistant to deer.

Available from Native Plant Growers
Size: 3-6 Feet Tall x 3 Feet Wide
Bloom: Red / July to Frost
Uses: Mid-Back Border, Shade, Wetland

USDA Zones: 7-11
Sun: Sun to Full Shade
Soil: Woodland, Tolerant Drought, Sandy, Clay

BLACKFOOT DAISY

Blackfoot Daisy is a charming, long-blooming plant with showy white flowers that look almost like White Zinnias and last throughout the growing season. Blackfoot Daisy is sold as a perennial, but in my experience, it is best considered an annual, because it frequently does not come back—or maybe it is just late. It will often self-seed, but the timing is often too late in spring for me, as I've already planted new replacements.

The plant grows neatly, spreads as much as two to three feet, and boasts tiny daisy-like flowers throughout the season—a real show-stopper! Blackfoot Daisy is drought-tolerant, deer resistant, and virtually maintenance free. Thriving in heat, it's perfectly happy surrounded by gravel or concrete. With its honey-scented flower heads, Blackfoot Daisy, or Rock Daisy as it is also known, is a worthwhile plant, even if you need to replant it each year.

Available from Native Plant Growers
Size: 8-12 Inches Tall x 24 Inches Wide
Bloom: White, Yellow Center / March to November
Uses: Ground Cover, Rock Garden

USDA Zones: 4-8
Sun: Full Sun
Soil: Limestone, Sand, Well-Drained

Monarda fistulosa
WILD BERGAMOT, BEE BALM

       The flowers of the Bee Balm plant are strikingly interesting with an open, daisy-like shape with extruding tubular petals. Similar to other members of the mint family, what appears to be a large single flower is actually a cluster of small blossoms that are perfectly designed for butterflies and hummingbirds. Bee Balm is of a size that makes it best suited for a back-of-the-border planting with something added to the front to cover the feet of the plant, which can get somewhat leggy.

       This plant is susceptible to several diseases including powdery mildew, but does well with good drainage and air circulation. Bee Balm can be deadheaded to prolong the bloom period and prevent self-seeding. Also, dividing the plant every 3-4 years may increase flowering.

       Eastern Bee Balm (M. bradburiana), is similar to Wild Bergamot but grows to only 1-2 feet tall and blooms earlier in May. Both varieties are resistant to deer and rabbits.

Available from Native Plant Growers	**USDA Zones:** 4-9
Size: 2-4 Feet Tall x 2-3 Feet Wide	**Sun:** Full Sun to Part Sun
Bloom: Lavender, Pink / July to September	**Soil:** Rich, Moisture-Retentive
Uses: Accent, Back Border, Naturalize, Rain Garden	

Oenothera lindheimeri

GAURA, BEE BLOSSOM, or WAND FLOWER

Native Gaura is an extremely tough, drought-tolerant plant that blooms all summer with the daintiest of flowers. A member of the evening primrose family, the deep-rooted plant has a taproot that can make it difficult to transplant Gaura after only one year. Once established this is a very drought tolerant plant.

Also known as Wandflower and Whirling Butterfly for the way the small flowers dance amongst the long, pinkish stems. Pruning the plant's wayward stems not only maintains its shape but also encourages new flowering. As with all plants, it is important to put Gaura in the right spot in order to avoid excessive pruning of flower buds.

'Siskiyou Pink' is a more compact, hardy pink cultivar that is much showier than the standard white.

Gaura is somewhat resistant to deer and rabbit browsing.

Available from Good Nurseries
Size: 2-4 Feet Tall x 2-4 Feet Wide
Bloom: White, Pink / May to September
Uses: Accent, Borders, Massing, Rock Gardens

USDA Zones: 5-9
Sun: Full Sun
Soil: Dry to Medium

Oenothera macrocarpa

MISSOURI EVENING PRIMROSE

Missouri Evening Primrose is a plant that I am frequently asked about since it is so striking when in bloom. It makes a beautiful 10-12" tall groundcover that becomes covered in large 3-4" lemon-yellow flowers for much of the year. I've always been confused as to why it is also called Missouri Evening Primrose, and is purported to be an evening bloomer. Mine have always opened during the day and stay open until evening—one flower per day, but lots of flowers, and quite fragrant.

This is a drought tolerant, spreading plant with shiny, narrow, grey-green leaves with prominent center veins. It is easy to transplant babies in spring and move them around or gift them to friends. Even with so many of them, I still love it. Bees, moths, and hummingbirds also love this plant.

You can deadhead the flowers to reduce reseeding.

Available from Native Plant Growers
Size: 8-12 Inches Tall x 24 Inches Wide
Bloom: Lemon yellow /April through August
Uses: Borders, Groundcover, Rock Garden

USDA Zones: 3-7
Sun: Full Sun
Soil: Limestone, Sand, dry, well-drained

Packera obovata

ROUNDLEAF RAGWORT, GOLDEN GROUNSEL

Roundleaf Ragwort makes a beautiful groundcover that thrives and blooms in deep shade. Its long bloom time begins in early spring about the same time that the dogwoods bloom. Flat-topped clusters of bright yellow, daisy-like flowers grow on stems that are 18 inches above the plant. For the rest of the year, this plant makes a beautiful, low-growing evergreen groundcover that is four- to six-inch tall, as long as some moisture is present.

Roundleaf Ragwort will spread, and some might even call it invasive, so placement is important. Once established, the plant naturalizes into large colonies by reseeding and through stolons, or runners and creates an evergreen groundcover.

Golden Ragwort, Packera aurea, is a similar plant, with flowers bloom on 2-3' stalks.

Available from Native Plant Growers
Size: Leaves: 4" tall; flowers 1-2 feet tall
Bloom: Yellow /April to May
Uses: Ground Cover, Naturalize, Rain Garden

USDA Zones: 3-8
Sun: Full Sun to Shade
Soil: Moist, Well-Drained

WILD QUININE

Wild Quinine is seen in Oklahoma's prairies, meadows, and open woodlands. It is a large (1-3' tall) bushy plant with clusters of small white, daisy-like flowers that look like cauliflower from a distance during the summer. It is a plant that will grow in a clump in dry areas in full sun with a deep tap root making it very drought tolerant. It can be introduced into prairies or meadows for interest and to provide food for bees, wasps and other insects. This is a low maintenance plant that needs no irrigation or fertilizer.

This plant makes a great dried cut flower and is deer-resistant.

Available from Native Plant Growers
Size: 3-5 Feet Tall x 2-3 Feet Wide
Bloom: White / June to September
Uses: Cottage garden, rock garden, naturalize, cut flower

USDA Zones: 4-8
Sun: Full Sun to Part Sun
Soil: Prefers fertile loam; will tolerate sandy, rocky or clay soils

FOXGLOVE BEARDTONGUE

Penstemon or Foxglove Beardtongue is a genus of about 250 species of herbaceous perennials that live in a variety of habitats, and many hybrids of this plant have been developed. The straight species has white flowers, although others have violet, blue, red and are quite showy for a good month during late spring. Some cultivars have burgundy colored foliage, making the plant showy for a long time in the landscape. My limited experience is that these cultivars are not as tough as the straight species with green-leaves. The colored leaves may also confuse the pollinators.

Beard Tongue is great for clay loam and in areas with poor drainage. It grows well in full sun but will tolerate dry shade. It attracts long-tongued bees and hummingbirds and the flowers work well as a cut flower. This plant is resistant to deer and rabbits.

Available from Native Plant Growers   **USDA Zones:** 3-8
Size: 3-5 Feet Tall x 1.5-2 Feet Wide   **Sun:** Full Sun to Part Sun
Bloom: White-Pink / May to July   **Soil:** Dry to Wet, Clay Loam
Uses: Accent, Borders, Cottage Gardens, Rain Gardens

WILD BLUE PHLOX

Wild Blue Phlox, also known as Woodland Phlox, grows and blooms well in part sun to shady areas. This fragrant wildflower is often found in woods with rich, acidic soils and along streams. This plant attracts many butterfly species.

In the spring, Wild Blue Phlox is covered with beautiful, slightly fragrant and showy blue flowers. The plant can spread and form colonies as stems along the ground take root. However, Wild Blue Phlox is not overly aggressive, and unwanted seedlings can be easily pulled, or better, transplanted.

Cutting back stems after flowering can help control powdery mildew. This plant draws little interest from deer, although rabbits seem to find the roots quite tasty.

Available from Native Plant Growers
Size: 8-12 Inches Tall x 8-12 Inches Wide
Bloom: Rose/Lavender, Violet/Blue / April to May
Uses: Ground Cover, Shady Border, Woodland

USDA Zones: 2-10
Sun: Part Sun to Shade
Soil: Rich, Well-Drained, Moist

TALL GARDEN PHLOX

Surprisingly, tall Garden Phlox is the same old-fashioned phlox your grandmother kept in her garden. Who knew it was native to Oklahoma? The plant spreads in wet locations but is not difficult to control. It will also grow in sun and partial shade as well as in rich garden soil. This plant does require regular watering, so it is not suitable for dry areas. All of the varieties of garden phlox that I have grown have been from divisions from a friend or neighbor. This plant will reseed itself.

Many cultivars are available in a variety of flower colors, including white, lavender, pink, rose, red, and attractive bicolored flowers, which are all quite fragrant. Cultivars resistant to powdery mildew should be selected, and good air circulation is a must. Some of the taller cultivars may need staking.

Readily Available   **USDA Zones:** 4-8
Size: 2-4 Feet Tall x 2-3 Feet Wide   **Sun:** Full Sun to Part Sun
Bloom: Pink, Purple, White / July to September   **Soil:** Well-Drained, Medium,
Uses: Naturalizing Wet Sites, Border, Shade Gardens   Moist

DOWNY PHLOX, PRAIRIE PHLOX

Prairie Phlox has showy, fragrant, tubular, one-half-inch long pink to pale purple flowers loosely packed in clusters. Butterflies and bees love the intensely fragrant flowers that bloom for about three to four weeks in the early spring. Often called Downy Phlox because of the hairy-like appearance of its stems and leaves, the plant has a taproot that sends up several stems from the same root system. This plant has few insect problems, and good resistance to powdery mildew.

Native to open woods and prairies, Prairie Phlox is fairly drought-tolerant. It attracts bees and butterflies and is deer resistant. This plant is easy to grow from seed.

Available from Native Plant Growers
Size: 1-2 Feet Tall x 1-1.5 Feet Wide
Bloom: Pink to Pale Purple / May to June
Uses: Borders, Prairie, Rock Gardens, Wild Gardens

USDA Zones: 4-9
Sun: Full Sun to Part Sun
Soil: Sandy, Rocky Loam, Well-Drained

Phlox subulata

CREEPING PHLOX

I love this plant as it is one of the signs that spring has finally arrived! Creeping phlox is a familiar, creeping plant, which flowers about the same time as spring bulbs. Showy flowers carpet the plant and last about two to four weeks.

This is a very common ornamental ground cover, which comes in many flower colors, including red, white, blue, rose, lavender, or pink. After the bloom disappears, the leaves remain green, although somewhat subdued, for most of the year. Creeping Phlox has evergreen, needlelike foliage and is tolerant of summer drought, heat, and compacted soils.

To promote more dense growth, cut back the stems of the plant after flowering. This plant will benefit from supplemental watering during dry periods.

Readily Available
Size: 4-8 Inches Tall x 12-24 Inches Wide
Bloom: Blue, Pink, Red / March to April
Uses: Border Edges, Ground Cover, Rock Gardens

USDA Zones: 3-9
Sun: Full Sun
Soil: Well-Drained Rich or Sandy

Another plant with a fun name is Frogfruit, an outstanding low-growing ground cover with miniature flowers just about the right size to be appreciated by the frog. It flourishes in partial shade, and the tiny blooms attract tiny bees as well as butterflies. Although the flowers are small, it flowers most of the year.

Frogfruit prefers damp areas. However, it also grows well in full sun and dry shade. Frogfruit can spread to cover a large area and is appropriately used under existing trees or open spaces where it will have room to grow. The plant does not take foot traffic well.

I have had a large patch of Frogfruit growing as a 'lawn' area in full sun, where it receives no irrigation or fertilization. I mow it 2-3 times a year, just to keep it from overtaking other plants. It can be an aggressive spreader in full sun—not a good one for small spaces. It will tolerate drought and flooding.

Available from Native Plant Growers
Size: 1-2 Feet Tall x 2 Feet Wide
Bloom: White /April to October
Uses: Ground Cover, Hanging Baskets

USDA Zones: 6-10
Sun: Full Sun to Part Sun
Soil: Any

SMOOTH SOLOMON'S SEAL

Tired of snails eating your hostas in the summer? Consider replacing them with Solomon's Seal, a perfect plant for shaded areas with cool, rich, and moist soils, ensuring a snail-free plant.

Solomon's Seal is beautiful, with a graceful arching form, a delicate leaf, small fragrant flowers and showy blue-black berries that both dangle from the leaf. Adding to that, it has a lovely lemon-yellow fall color. Something beautiful for the entire year! This plant has no serious disease or pest problems and the flowers will attract various bees and hummingbirds.

Available from Native Plant Growers
Size: 2-3 Feet Tall x 12 Inches Wide
Bloom: Yellowish-green to White/
May-June
Uses: Border Edges, Woodland Garden, Shade Gardens
This plant is edible, but the berries are poisonous to humans.

USDA Zones: 3-9
Sun: Partial - Full Shade
Soil: Rich, soil with high organic matter, moist with good drainage

SLENDER MOUNTAIN MINT, NARROWLEAF MOUNTAIN MINT

Mountain Mint grows well in dry areas, clay soil, and even in rocky soils. The plant has silvery-green needle-like foliage and showy white flowers that are loved by bees and butterflies. Crushing its flowers and leaves emits a pleasant minty scent.

An easily grown, upright, shrubby perennial, Mountain Mint can be vigorous and can spread, but I wouldn't consider it aggressive. This drought tolerant plant is tolerant of any soil type.

Deer may browse the leaves, and the seeds attract various animals, though the seeds are too small to attract birds. Leaves rubbed on your skin are said to repel mosquitoes and can also be used in teas or as a spice for cooking.

Available from Native Plant Growers
Size: 2-3 Feet Tall x 2-3 Feet Wide
Bloom: White / July to September
Uses: Cut Flowers, Naturalize, Rain Garden

USDA Zones: 4-8
Sun: Full Sun to Part Sun
Soil: Any

MEXICAN HAT

Named for its distinctive sombrero-shaped flower, Mexican Hat blooms from May to July, but blooms can extend through September if there is plenty of moisture. The tall, leafless flower stalk can reach three feet, typically topping out at about half that height. The rest of the year the foliage is light, lacy, and attractive.

A fast-growing wildflower, Mexican Hat is not fussy about soils and is easy to grow from seed. Seeding is most successful if planted in fall, although they may be seeded in spring. The plant is frequently seeded into lawns and on the side of the highway, thriving so long as it has good seed-to-soil contact. Mexican Hat is perennial, but a harsh winter may kill it off. It has a deep taproot, making it very drought tolerant.

Available from Native Plant Growers
Size: 1-3 Feet Tall x 1 Foot Wide
Bloom: Yellow, Orange / May to August
Uses: Border Front, Massing, Naturalize

USDA Zones: 3-9
Sun: Full Sun
Soil: Dry to Medium Well-Drained

Rudbeckia fulgida

BLACK-EYED SUSAN, ORANGE CONEFLOWER

There seem to be so many 'Black-eyed Susans' that I'm never sure if I have planted the best one. They are all similar with 2-3" diameter daisy-like flowers with yellow-orange petals surrounding a dark eye center: R. hirta (3' tall annual or short-lived perennial); R. missouriensis (2-3' tall perennial); and R. fulgida (up to 4' tall perennial) are probably just a few examples. Oklahoma growers recommend R. fulgida, and I trust that they know best.

One thing is for certain: when the plant is in bloom, you can't miss it. Members of the aster family, Black-Eyed Susans are all beautiful, with long flowering times and much loved by pollinators. Black-Eyed Susan blooms continually through the summer months and will seed, spread, and overtake smaller plants

Plant or sow seeds directly into the garden in the fall or after the last spring frost. Highly drought and heat tolerant, this plant is considered deer resistant.

Available from Good Nurseries	**USDA Zones:** 3-7
Size: 2-3 Feet Tall x 1-2 Feet Wide	**Sun**: Full Sun to Part Sun
Bloom: Orange, Yellow with Black	**Soil**: All But Poorly Drained, Best
Center / June to September	Sandy
Uses: Cut Flowers, Ground Cover, Massing, Meadows	

Rudbeckia maxima

GIANT CONEFLOWER

Giant Coneflower is the plant that my neighbors ask me about most often. Big and showy, the plant easily reaches six feet tall when in bloom. The large, grayish-green leaves are interesting for most of the growing season. The seed heads stay showy well into the winter, providing a seed source for goldfinches and maintaining a structure in the landscape when other plants aren't doing much. So, resist cutting the seed heads back until the following spring. The plant creates a real focal point in the landscape and makes a good companion plant to Tall Coreopsis, (C. tripteris), which has a similar height and flower color.

The plant is pest resistant and foliage is unpalatable to deer and other herbivores. It was discovered by the English botanist Thomas Nuttall in 1816 near the Red River in what was then Oklahoma Territory.

Available from Native Plant Growers	**USDA Zones:** 4-9
Size: 5-7 Feet Tall x 3-4 Feet Wide	**Sun**: Full Sun to Part Sun
Bloom: Yellow with Brown Center / June to July	**Soil**: Tolerates Most, Best in Well-Drained, Rich
Uses: Accent, Back Border, Cut Flower	

Rudbeckia subtomentosa
SWEET CONEFLOWER

Sweet Coneflower offers a dazzling display of golden yellow flowers with dark brown, dome-shaped centers in the mid-summer—making this plant a native superstar. Resilient and long-lived, this plant flowers in late summer, between the seasons of many other flowering plants. Foliage is medium green in a tidy basal clump from which the strong, multiples of flowering stems arise.

This upright perennial can reach nearly six feet in height, and can topple over if spoiled with too much water or fertilizer. Also known as Fragrant Coneflower, its yellow daisy-like flowers emit a subtle, sweet, anise-like scent. The Sweet Coneflower is more long-lived than its sisters, Black-Eyed Susan and Brown-Eyed Susan. This is also great as a cut flower.

Available from Native Plant Growers
Size: 5-7 Feet Tall x 3-4 Feet Wide
Bloom: Yellow with Brown Center /
June to July
Uses: Accent, Borders, Naturalize, Rain Garden

USDA Zones: 4-9
Sun: Full Sun to Part Sun
Soil: Moist to Wet, Clay

Salvia azurea

BLUE SAGE

Azure Sage produces bright, azure blue, two-lipped flowers that bloom for long periods toward the end of summer on a plant that is 3-5' tall. This is an easy to grow plant that will flop over if placed in rich soils. So, avoid fertilizer and consider pinching the plant back in late spring to make a sturdier plant or be prepared to stake it.

Native to prairies, meadows, and pastures on sandy soils, Azure Sage thrives in dry conditions. Like other salvias, it will emit a strong scent when rubbed. This plant attracts butterflies and hummingbirds and is deer resistant.

Available from Native Plant Growers   **USDA Zones:** 5-9
Size: 3-5 Feet Tall x 2-4 Feet Wide   **Sun**: Full Sun-Partial Sun
Bloom: Sky Blue / July to October   **Soil**: Well drained, clay, loam, sand
Uses: Accent, Cottage Garden, Borders, Naturalize

Salvia greggii
AUTUMN SAGE

I loved this plant before I knew it was a native and before I understood the importance of providing for our pollinators. Autumn Sage is a beautifully compact and well-behaved plant that starts blooming in spring and reaches a crescendo in the fall, hence its name, Autumn Sage.

Salvia greggi blooms in many colors: white, salmon, peppermint, purple, and orange; however, the 'Pink Preference' cultivar stands out for its colorful pink-red flowers that, unlike others, last a full season. The only maintenance required for this plant is to cut it back to about a foot tall in the early spring, which allows it to maintain a neat shape at two-to three-feet tall throughout the year. Hummingbirds absolutely love this plant and can frequently be seen hovering around, grabbing some of the plant's ample and sweet nectar.

Readily Available　　　　　　　　**USDA Zones:** 5-9
Size: 1-3 Feet Tall x 3 Feet Wide　　**Sun**: Full Sun
Bloom: Orange, Pink-Red, Purple, White　　**Soil**: Well-Drained
/ March to November
Uses: Accent, Herb Garden, Mid-Border, Foundation Shrub

HOARY SKULLCAP

What you really want to know about this plant is what kind of name is Hoary Skull Cap?

Apparently, the 'skull' part is from the botanical name scutellaria, which means 'little shield' and refers to the flower shape and 'hoary' refers to tiny hairs on the leaves and stems. Someone could have done better with naming this charming little plant.

It is a lovely, low-growing plant that is found in rocky open woods, woodland edges and shaded roadsides. It has interesting bluish-purple flowers in 6" spikes at the end of the stems that attract bees, moths and songbirds. This is a good flowering plant for shady areas.

These plants have bitter-tasting leaves and so are usually ignored by deer and rabbits.

Available from Native Plant Growers	**USDA Zones:** 5-9
Size: 2-3 Feet Tall x 1-2 Feet Wide	**Sun:** Part Sun-Shade
Bloom: Purple, Blue, White / June-September	**Soil:** Rich acid soils and sands; dry to moist
Uses: Borders, shade gardens, accent, mass planting, xeric gardens	

CUP PLANT

Cup Plant is a coarse-textured, sunflower-like native plant that naturally occurs in woodlands, thickets, meadows, and near streams or ponds. Tall, with cup-forming leaves that hold water and attract birds and frogs, the plant is best suited to wet areas and partial shade, although it will tolerate some drought once established. Impressive yellow flowers grow as large as three to four inches in diameter with dark yellow centers.

If the plant likes its location, it will reseed and spread, popping up everywhere in the landscape. Cup Plant needs very little care, which makes it a great option for a back-of-the-border planting. The plant attracts a high number of all kinds of bees and blooms into September.

Available from Native Plant Growers **USDA Zones:** 3-9
Size: 4-8 Feet Tall x 1-3 Feet Wide **Sun:** Full Sun
Bloom: Yellow, Dark Center / July to September **Soil:** Clay or Wet
Uses: Back Border, Meadows, Naturalize, Rain Garden

BLUE-EYED GRASS

This perfectly named plant is just the cutest! It looks like a clumping grass, with tiny, star-shaped, blue blossoms at the end of it. But it is small, only 10-12" tall, so give consideration to a place it where it will be appreciated.

This is actually a member of the Iris family and the leaves resemble the overlapping fans of the iris. Typically found on woodland edges, moist meadows, and roadsides, Blue-eyed Grass can spread through underground rhizomes or by seed, but it is not a big problem. I wish mine would spread more!

A great plant for tiny bees and butterflies.

Available from Native Plant Growers
Size: 6-8 Inches Tall x 6inches Wide
Bloom: Blue / May, June
Uses: Groundcover, edging plant, naturalize, accent

USDA Zones: 4-10
Sun: Full Sun to Partial Shade
Soil: Medium-Wet to Medium-Dry

GOLDENROD

Goldenrod will stop traffic in the fall when it is completely covered with foot-long, bright yellow-gold blooms. The most common species can easily reach five-feet tall and can live in multiple soil types.

In the garden, goldenrod can quickly take over, spreading by both seed or rhizomes. It needs a large area to spread. I have a neighbor that planted one plant last year in a small bed surrounded by lawn. Now he has at least 20 in that bed with the surrounding mown lawn preventing any newcomers. Not a bad way to have a low-maintenance bed that is ideal for pollinators.

The plant is very easy to grow, tolerant of a wide range of soils, heat, and drought. There are over a hundred species of Goldenrod native to the United States. Most of them prefer dry sun, but look for species that match your soil and sun conditions. The plant gets a bad rap as the cause for fall hay fever, but it just happens to bloom at the same time as ragweed, which is the actual cause. Goldenrod is one of the top twelve plants for monarchs.

Available from Native Plant Growers
Size: 2-6 Feet Tall x 2-3 Feet Wide
Bloom: Yellow-Gold / July to November
Uses: Accent, Border, Massing

USDA Zones: 3-8
Sun: Full Sun
Soil: Dry to Moderately, Moist, Well-Drained

ASTERS

Asters lay low for most of the year, but then comes September, and these little green shrubs burst into bright purple with one- to two-inch-wide flowers covering the entire plant. Asters provide far better fall color than mums and are easy to grow. The plant also provides a critical fall nectar source for pollinators, especially monarchs as the butterflies stock up for their fall migration to Mexico.

Above, Aromatic Aster (S. oblongifolium) grows in a compact mound standing two- to four-feet tall. The New England Aster (S. novae-angliae) is taller, sometimes reaching five feet in height. There are over 100 species of symphyotrichum, with colorful fall flowers and that can reach six foot in height.

Plants can be cut back before July to improve their shape but cutting back later will risk losing buds needed to produce flowers.

The plant is listed as one of the top twelve plants for monarchs.

Available from Good Nurseries
Size: 2-6 Feet Tall x 2-4 Feet Wide
Bloom: Blue, Purple, Pink, White/August to October
Uses: Borders, Massing, Naturalizing

USDA Zones: 4-8
Sun: Full Sun to Partial sun
Soil: Medium, Tolerates Clay, Rich

SPIDERWORT

Spiderwort has delicate, blue-purple, three-petaled flowers up to one-and-a-half-inches in diameter. Blooming in the morning and only for one day, buds will bloom in succession from May to July. The dark-green, arching, grass-like leaves extend about a foot or two from the plant, which tends to grow in clumps.

The Ohio Spiderwort (T. ohiensis), is larger, growing two to three feet in full sun to part shade and in dry soil while Spider Lily, T. virginiana, is smaller, reaching to one- to three-feet tall in part to full shade in clay soil. Many other species are available, offering a choice of sizes and a variety of purple-blue flowers.

You can cut the plant back after blooming if you want to enjoy more attractive new growth. Spiderwort is an easily grown, resilient plant that does best in partial shade.

Available from Native Plant Growers
Size: 1-3 Feet Tall x 12-18 Inches Wide
Bloom: Blue-Violet / May to July
Uses: Border, Naturalize, Shade Garden, Woodlands, Insects, birds

USDA Zones: 4-9
Sun: Part Sun to Shade
Soil: Various, Moist to Dry

GOLDEN CROWNBEARD, COWPEN DAISY

Golden Crownbeard is one of the best nectar plants for bees, butterflies, and all kinds of insects. An annual, it is planted by seed and will reseed. It is often found on disturbed ground and along roadsides.

Crownbeard, also known as Cowpen Daisy, has yellow daisy-like flowerheads with gray-green toothed leaves. The plant is drought tolerant but will tend to flop or become messy with too much water or nutrients. This plant is excellent for reclamation or disturbed areas and in pollinator conservation mixtures. Site Crownbeard carefully as it will reseed prolifically.

To harvest seed, allow seedheads to dry on the plants before removal. Plant seeds in November for following spring blooms. Native Americans used the plant to treat skin ailments. A member of the aster family, it is also highly deer resistant.

Available from Native Seed Producers　　**USDA Zones**: 2-9
Size: 1-4 Feet Tall x 1-3 Feet Wide　　**Sun**: Full Sun
Bloom: Yellow / June to October　　**Soil**: Sandy or Limestone, Alkaline
Uses: Accent, Ground Cover, Massing Naturalize

NARROWLEAF IRONWEED, THREADLEAF IRONWEED

Narrowleaf Ironweed, a mounding perennial wildflower with fine-textured leaves, is found on rocky floodplains and rock outcrops in Oklahoma and Arkansas.

Typically two feet tall and three feet wide, this long-lived herbaceous perennial has a deep tap-root and stems that originate from a dense crown. Its leaves are 1/8 inch wide by 3-inch-long, and cover the unbranched stems from top to bottom.

From September through October the plant is topped with small purple flowers, attracting a wide range of butterflies.

The 'Iron Butterfly' variety is stands out for its vigorous growth, compact habit (2-3' tall), smaller leaves and tiny, showy flowers. I have this plant in my yard and just love the fine texture and tiny, deep purple flowers that cover the plant in the fall. It is just beautiful! Deer Resistant.

Available from Native Plant Growers
Size: 2-3 Feet Tall and Wide
Bloom: Red or Purple / September to October
Uses: Accent, Massing, Cottage Gardens, Perennial Borders

USDA Zones: 4-9
Sun: Full Sun to Partial Shade
Soil: Moist-Wet

GOLDEN ALEXANDER

In the parsley family, Golden Alexander is considered a short-lived perennial, but since it reseeds it will stay in an area. Golden Alexanders have beautiful yellow flowers, which are attractive to many beneficial pollinators. After flowering, the seeds are showy, by hanging on in the same intricate pattern as the flowers.

I've always noticed that there are two kinds of leaves on this plant: the lower leaves are divided into threes twice while the upper leaves are divided once. This is a good way to identify the plant when it's not in flower. This plant prefers moist to wet soils, but will tolerate drought.

Zizia aurea is a host plant for the Black Swallowtail and the Ozark Swallowtail butterflies, in addition to supporting many small bees, flies and beetles.

Available from Native Plant Growers
Size: 1-3 Feet Tall and 1' Wide
Bloom: Yellow / May-August
Uses: Accent, Cottage Gardens, Perennial Borders Cut Flowers

USDA Zones: 3-9
Sun: Full Sun to Partial Shade
Soil: Prefers Clay-loam, rocky or gravely soil

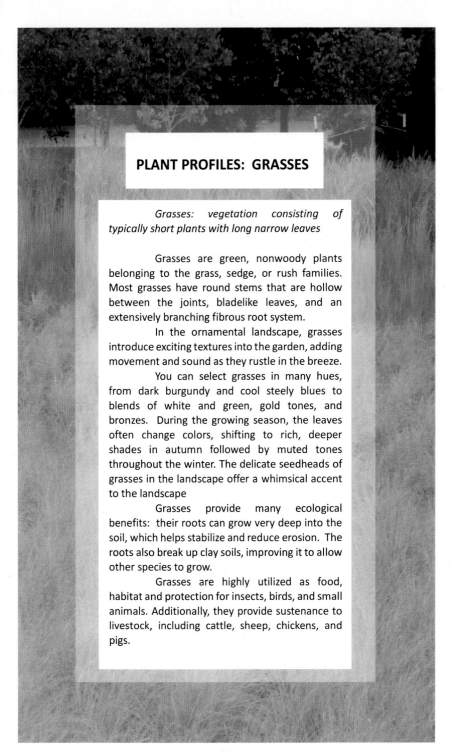

PLANT PROFILES: GRASSES

Grasses: vegetation consisting of typically short plants with long narrow leaves

Grasses are green, nonwoody plants belonging to the grass, sedge, or rush families. Most grasses have round stems that are hollow between the joints, bladelike leaves, and an extensively branching fibrous root system.

In the ornamental landscape, grasses introduce exciting textures into the garden, adding movement and sound as they rustle in the breeze.

You can select grasses in many hues, from dark burgundy and cool steely blues to blends of white and green, gold tones, and bronzes. During the growing season, the leaves often change colors, shifting to rich, deeper shades in autumn followed by muted tones throughout the winter. The delicate seedheads of grasses in the landscape offer a whimsical accent to the landscape

Grasses provide many ecological benefits: their roots can grow very deep into the soil, which helps stabilize and reduce erosion. The roots also break up clay soils, improving it to allow other species to grow.

Grasses are highly utilized as food, habitat and protection for insects, birds, and small animals. Additionally, they provide sustenance to livestock, including cattle, sheep, chickens, and pigs.

Andropogon gerardii

BIG BLUESTEM

One of the dominant grasses of the tallgrass prairie, Big Bluestem has attractive gray-to-blue-green foliage during the summer, transitioning to red hues in the fall and finally reddish-bronze after the frost.

The flowers include distinct three-parted clusters that resemble turkey feet. A fine ornamental grass in dry areas, Big Bluestem has a root system that runs as much as eight-feet deep, making it very drought tolerant. If too much water or fertilizer is available, the plant will tend to get top-heavy and fall over, losing its attractive vertical shape. This plant can be aggressive in the garden, spreading by seed or rhizomes, so give it a lot of room.

Big Bluestem is the larval host for many species of butterflies and it is known as the "ice-cream grass" for livestock and wildlife because they often will eat it before any others. Both birds and mammals use Big Bluestem for nesting and cover in summer and winter.

Available from Native Plant Growers
Size: 5-8 Feet Tall x 2-3 Feet Wide
Bloom: Purplish Red / September to February
Uses: Accent, Massing, Back Border, Erosion Control

USDA Zones: 4-10
Sun: Full Sun
Soil: Tolerates All, Prefers Dry Infertile

Andropogon glomeratus

BUSHY BLUESTEM

CREDIT: NATIVE PLANTS NURSERY

Bushy Bluestem is a vertical growing grass, similar to Little Bluestem but with an extra feature: groupings of flowers called spikelets at the top of the plant. The image on this page shows the visual effect of the fluffy flower heads. It is very easy to see, and distinguish this grass from any other.

Bushy Blustem is found within moist or semi-moist soils in full sun. It has the coloration of Little Bluestem with a grey-blue in summer and copper in winter.

Seeds are eaten by birds and small mammals while the plants provide nesting materials for birds and cover for small mammals.

Like other warm-season grasses, this plant has extreme flammability and should not be planted near structures.

Available from Native Plant Growers	**USDA Zones:** 7-9
Size: 2-4 Feet Tall x 2-3 Feet Wide	**Sun**: Full Sun
Bloom: White, Brown / August to November	**Soil**: Prefers Moist
Uses: Prairie plantings, rain gardens, bog gardens, near streams or ponds	

Bouteloua curtipendula

SIDEOATS GRAMA

Sideoats Grama is a gray-green, clumping, warm-season grass that is also one of the toughest and showiest native grasses available. It is topped with slender, oat-like flowers that distinctly drape along one side of the stem; hence, the name "sideoats." In fall, the foliage and flowers turn rich shades of orange and bronze. A tough, deep-rooted grass, Sideoats Grama was once the main grass of the shortgrass prairie.

This grass is one of the most important of range grass species - relished by livestock and deer through the summer and fall. Sideoats Grama is credited with revitalizing the land after the Dust Bowl of the 1930s.

This grass has great potential in the ornamental landscape as it is not as aggressive as others. Sideoats Grama contributes well to smaller gardens, but it will still flop over if given even a little too much care.

Available from Native Plant Growers **USDA Zones:** 3-9
Size: 18-24 Inches Tall x 12-18 Inches Wide **Sun:** Full Sun
Bloom: Purplish-Tan / July to September **Soil:** Any, Drought Tolerant
Uses: Borders, Erosion Control, Massing, Rocky Slopes

Bouteloua dactyloides

BUFFALO GRASS

Buffalo Grass is the grass that we should be using as a turfgrass in Oklahoma if we could go back in time before Bermuda grass invaded the United States. This grass is a low-growing, sod-forming, warm-season grass that will tolerate mowing. Its exceptional drought tolerance allows it to enter dormancy without dying during severe dry spells. A gray-green, fine-textured grass, it was originally an instrumental part of the shortgrass prairie and thrives particularly well in the dry clay soils of western and central Oklahoma.

Because Buffalo Grass is slow to establish, it cannot compete with the aggressive Bermuda grass that has been commonly planted throughout the state. To establish Buffalo Grass, the planting field must be completely cleared of the former, which is difficult to do. While seeding is an option, quicker establishment can be achieved through plug planting, spacing them six to twelve inches on center. There are several improved cultivars are available for better color.

Available from Some Sod Producers	**USDA Zones:** 3-9
Size: 4-6 Inches Tall	**Sun:** Full Sun
Bloom: Green, Not Showy /April to December	**Soil:** Prefers Slightly
Uses: Accent, Ground Cover, Turfgrass	Clayey

Bouteloua gracilis

BLUE GRAMA

Blue Grama has a light blue-green, fine-textured foliage with flowers that are like horizontal eyelashes in a nice chartreuse color that ages to blonde seedheads in fall. The species can also be maintained as a weather-resistant, deep-rooted, warm-season turfgrass in full sun.

The cultivars, 'Blonde Ambition' and 'Hachita', are the most showy and vigorous, reaching thirty inches tall while in bloom. This is an excellent choice for an ornamental setting with flowers that compete with any alien grass. The blooms extend as much as a foot taller than the main plant and are very showy from a distance. Blue Grama's consistent size makes it ideal for mass planting while also serving as an impressive standalone accent.

On the shortgrass prairie, Blue Grama ranks with Buffalo Grass as one of the most important forage plants and can survive on just seven inches of water per year!

Available from Good Nurseries　　　　　　**USDA Zones:** 3-10
Size: 8-30 Inches Tall x 24 Inches Wide　　**Sun**: Full Sun
Bloom: White, Blonde / June to August　　**Soil**: Sand or Clay
Uses: Accent, Filler, Lawns, Massing

SEDGES

There are more than five thousand species of grass-like or rush-like plants in the family Cyperaceae worldwide, with more than a hundred species of Carex or native Sedge that look and act like grasses. Sedges thrive across many habitats, from sandy beaches to mountainous regions, woodlands, swamps, and marshes.

The plants are versatile, especially as to size and leaf color, and far too diverse to cover in detail here.

Most Sedges do much of their growing in the cooler seasons, going dormant in hot temperatures. The following pages show some of the most popular of the sedges available in Oklahoma.

PLAINS OVAL SEDGE, SHORT BEAK SEDGE

In the interest of science, I planted this sedge in a raised planter in full sun at my neighborhood entrance where it was hand watered exactly two times during its first year: once at planting and again during the middle of a 2-month drought. (OK, I admit, I'm lazy). At the end of that year, nearly everything in that planter died, except the Plains Oval Sedge. So, I am now convinced that sedges are, indeed, tolerant of Oklahoma's heat and drought.

This attractive, evergreen plant grows to about 12 inches high with tiny flowers and fine, narrow leaves. It grows in full sun to shade, swamps to raised planters, pastures and ditches. Where else is there? This is a beautiful, tough plant worthy of any site in Oklahoma. And its deer resistant too!

Available from Native Plant Growers   **USDA Zones:** 3-8
Size: 12 Inches Tall to 18-24 inches Wide   **Sun**: Full Sun to Partial Shade
Bloom: Green, Insignificant   **Soil**: Any
Uses: Ground Covers, Massing, Shade Gardens, Water Gardens

GRAY'S SEDGE

Gray's Sedge grows to about 2 feet tall, with ½" wide grass-like leaves, which are semi-evergreen. The seed heads are quite showy and look like 1-inch diameter round spikey stars with a striking greenish-yellow to brown color. Those fruits remain on the plant through the winter, making a nice accent against the evergreen foliage. This is a very tough plant, which can be planted in sun to partial shady areas and is great in woodlands and wetlands.

This plant reminds me of Liriope, or Lilyturf, which is native to China and Japan. But this Oklahoma native provides food for the larva of various butterflies.

Available from Native Plant Growers **USDA Zones:** 5-9
Size: 2-3 Feet Tall by 1.5-2 Feet Wide   **Sun:** Full Sun to Partial Shade
Bloom: Green, May-October   **Soil**: Moist, Fertile
Uses: Rain Garden, Bioswale, Ground Covers, Massing, Shade Gardens

Carex Pensylvanica

PENNSYLVANICA SEDGE

This sedge plant is native to dry woodland areas, growing in colonies with a creeping habit. This is one that could be used as a lawn alternative in dry shady areas. It can be mowed to maintain a 2" height, but does not handle foot traffic well. It could also be used as a green mulch, growing between other larger plants.

It grows to only 8 inches tall with a very fine texture. It is semi-evergreen and will die back in very cold temperatures.

Available from Native Plant Growers   **USDA Zones:** 3-7
Size: 6 Inches Tall to 12 inches Wide   **Sun**: Part Shade to Shade
Bloom: Green, Insignificant   **Soil**: Dry Loam
Uses: Ground Covers, Massing, Shade Gardens, Water Gardens

Carex texensis

Texas Sedge is a short, fine-textured sedge that grows to about 12 inches tall and could be used as a turf grass in moist, sandy soils. It can be mowed at a high setting if a neater appearance is desired.

This plant could also be used as a 'mulch plant', growing below and between other shrubs and perennials. It acts as green mulch or matrix plant that covers the ground between other shrubs and perennials, cutting down on maintenance needs by reducing mulching, weed growth and irrigation.

Texas Sedge will spread through rhizomes.

Available from Native Plant Growers   **USDA Zones:** 3-8
Size: 12 Inches Tall to 18-24 inches Wide   **Sun**: Full Sun to Partial Shade
Bloom: Green, Insignificant   **Soil**: Any
Uses: Ground Covers, Massing, Shade Gardens, Water Gardens

Northern Sea Oats is an attractive shade-loving grass that is native to streams and riverbanks, but also tolerant of sea spray (the latter obviously not a problem in Oklahoma). The attractive foliage is similar to bamboo and the seed heads rustle easily in the wind, adding movement to the garden. The flowers look like flat oats and emerge greenish-pink and then dry to a golden color, remaining showy well into winter. As the seedheads get large, the plant will often flop over from the weight. In fall, the foliage takes on a coppery color before turning brown in winter. Foliage can be sheared back in early spring to make way for new growth.

This grass will self-seed in moist soil, which is a good thing when used in the right location, but it can be problematic in manicured beds or near shaded lawns. It is drought tolerant once established.

Available from Native Plant Growers
Size: 2-3 Feet Tall x 2 Feet Wide
Bloom: Pinkish to Gold /August to September
Uses: Accent, Ground Covers, Massing

USDA Zones: 4-9
Sun: Part Sun to Shade
Soil: Any, as long as Moisture Present

PURPLE LOVE GRASS

A fine-textured, warm-season, bunch grass that loves dry, sandy soils and full sun, Purple Love Grass is tough and drought tolerant, even growing under black walnut trees and near roadsides that receive winter road salt. The seedheads bloom in midsummer with shades of purple, lending the landscape a reddish-purple haze. Planted by either seed or plugs, this perennial grass grows low to the ground in dense tufts.

Purple Love Grass will self-seed and is best used in masses or naturalized settings. Eventually, the foliage breaks off and floats around like a tumbleweed. The plant is sometimes confused with Love Grass (E. curvula), which is taller but originates from southern Africa and not native to this region.

Available: Native Plant Growers or Seed Suppliers **USDA Zones:** 5-9
Size: 1-2 Feet Tall x 1-2 Inches Wide **Sun**: Full Sun to Part
Bloom: Reddish-Purple / July to August Shade
Uses: Massing, Naturalize, Rock Garden **Soil**: Any but Prefers Dry
Sandy or Gravelly

PINK MUHLY GRASS

Muhly grasses offer stunning flowering accents for the warm season garden, with the bonus of Pink Muhly Grass being that it also attracts ladybugs. This plant has fine-textured, gray-green foliage that turns pink in the fall. There are several different cultivars, many of which are not cold-tolerant, so be careful to pick one that is hardy for your area. There are taller species for background plantings and others that grow much lower for massing. The plant needs full sun and dry conditions to look its best, and may suffer in shade or during wet summers.

Rose Muhly (M. reverchonhi), is shorter (twenty-four to thirty-inches tall) with similar fall flowering.

Pink Muhly Grass makes for an eye-popping addition to the garden and is drought tolerant too, although it can tolerate flooding for short spells. Muhly grasses will self-seed, but not to their detriment. It will not spread by rhizomes.

Available from Good Nurseries
Size: 2-4 Feet Tall x 2-4 Feet Wide
Bloom: Purple-Pink or White /
September to November
Uses: Accent, Borders, Massing, Meadows

USDA Zones: 5-9
Sun: Full Sun
Soil: Best in Sandy, Rocky, Well-Drained

MEXICAN FEATHER GRASS

Mexican Feather Grass is so widely planted that I fear it has become significantly overused in Oklahoma landscapes. Yet there is no denying its appeal. The plant has a graceful, fine, hairlike texture that weeps to the ground, especially when flowering with its silky, golden flowers.

Feather grass offers a great contrast to any other plant, but it is best used in mass plantings and in areas where the seedlings can't spread to natural plant ecosystems. That said, I won't plant this plant anymore, it self-seeds to its detriment and spreads into cracks in concrete and anywhere else the seeds contact the ground. If that isn't bad enough, it will then die back to the crown of the original plant. The grass has been classified as an invasive species in some regions. There are better grasses to use in your landscape that are less invasive and more beneficial for pollinators.

Readily Available   **USDA Zones:** 5-10
Size: 1-3 Feet Tall x 2 Feet Wide   **Sun**: Full Sun
Bloom: Silvery-White / June to September   **Soil**: Sandy, Clay, Average
Uses: Accent, Massing

Panicum virgatum
SWITCHGRASS

Distinguished by graceful, arching foliage, Switchgrass is an important species to plant along riverbanks and ponds, because its deep roots help to stabilize the banks. The plant can also tolerate the occasional flood. Away from water, Switchgrass makes for a well-mannered plant that will stay in place, becoming a thick clump of foliage. In the summer, hairy plumes of flowers top the foliage later turning into lacy seed heads. Its summer color is usually blue-green and turns to a warm yellow-orange in the winter.

A drought-tolerant and adaptable grass with many uses in the landscape, Switchgrass can be encouraged to produce new growth by cutting clumps back in early spring. Cultivars have been developed to distinguish colors and shapes: 'Heavy Metal' is 5' tall and 4' wide, 'Northwind' is 4' tall and 3' wide, while 'Shenandoah' is 3' tall with a burgundy color by mid-summer. 'Prairie Fire' is 4-5' tall with wine-red foliage in summer.

Available from Good Nurseries
Size: 3-8 Feet Tall x 4 Feet Wide
Bloom: Pinkish / July to August
Uses: Accent, Borders, Detention Ponds, Massing, Screening

USDA Zones: 3-9
Sun: Full Sun to Part Sun
Soil: Dry to Wet, Prefers Moist Sandy, Clay

LITTLE BLUESTEM

Little Bluestem is a distinctive grass that you see along roadways in Oklahoma in places where no one mows or maintains the grass. It has a strict upright growth and distinct coloration. In the summer, it has a bluish color, transforming to a beautiful salmon/copper color in the fall. While the stems of other grasses can become matted in winter, the stems of Little Bluestem remain boldly upright.

Little Bluestem's fibrous roots can extend five to eight feet below ground making it drought tolerant and a plant that is altogether tough-as-nails. If it starts to slump, you know it is being overwatered or over fertilized. It actually thrives on neglect. The grass is deer resistant and provides nesting shelter for bees, serving as the host plant for many skipper butterflies.

Both 'Blaze' and 'The Blues' are cultivars selected for superior summer and winter foliage colors.

Available from Native Plant Growers
Size: 2-4 Feet Tall x 1 Foot Wide
Bloom: Green / July to September
Uses: Accent, Ground Cover, Massing

USDA Zones: 3-10
Sun: Full Sun to Part Sun
Soil: Any, Except Wet or Boggy

INDIAN GRASS, YELLOW INDIANGRASS

Since 1972, Indian Grass has been the official state grass of Oklahoma, but for eons it was a major component of the North American tallgrass prairie. The grass grows in upright clumps with stiff, vertical flowering stems, topped with foot-long flower panicles that rise well above the foliage in the late summer. Indian Grass has blue-green foliage, contrasted by showy, golden flower plumes. The foliage turns first yellow and then orange in the fall.

A striking grass for accent or massing and useful in erosion control, Indian Grass is a warm-season perennial that provides excellent wildlife habitat as well as food for small mammals, deer and seed for birds. As with other native grasses, it is best to avoid too much irrigation or fertilization to ensure the best form. Some cultivars are available for improved color.

Available from Native Plant Growers
Size: 3-8 Feet Tall x 2-3 Feet Wide
Bloom: Golden / September to November
Uses: Accent, Back Border, Cut Flower, Massing

USDA Zones: 4-10
Sun: Full Sun to Part Sun
Soil: Any

PRAIRIE DROPSEED

Dropseed is a clump-forming, warm season grass native to the tall-grass prairie. It has elegant, fine-textured, medium-green leaves in an arching form, like a waterfall, before pink and brown-tinted flower heads emerge in mid to late summer. As fall approaches the foliage turns golden with orange hues, fading to a light bronze. It is known for its airy flowers and seed heads.

The plant is known to be slow-growing and slow to establish, but once established, Dropseed needs little care other than pulling, cutting, or burning off old foliage in late winter or early spring.

Prairie Dropseed has been described as the most handsome of all the prairie grasses. However, I will admit I have not been successful with it. I may just be impatient, but in my landscape, the plant has only grown six inches in the first year, and I have yet to see its beautiful arching form. I haven't given up! I'm told it is particularly striking when positioned so the flower and seed heads are backlit.

Available from Native Plant Growers	**USDA Zones:** 3-9
Size: 2-3 Feet Tall x 2-3 Feet Wide	**Sun:** Full Sun
Bloom: Green/Pink/Copper /	**Soil:** Average to Well-
August to October	Drained, Tolerates Clay
Uses: Ground Cover, Meadows, Rain Garden	

Okies for
MONARCHS

WHAT TO PLANT
12 Monarch Butterfly Plants Suitable Statewide

Visit **okiesformonarchs.org** for regional plant lists.

For optimum Monarch habitat, plant at least 10 milkweed plants, made up of two or more species, and several annual, biennial, or perennial plants that are in bloom sequentially or continuously during spring, summer and fall.

EARLY BLOOM

BUTTERFLY MILKWEED
Asclepias tuberosa, likes full sun. Blooms in the spring. Grows .75-1' ft. tall. High drought tolerance. Perennial. Host/nectar plant.

GREEN ANTELOPEHORN
Asclepias viridis, likes full sun. Blooms spring to late summer. Grows 1-2' tall. Medium water use. Perennial. Host/nectar plant.

GOLDEN CROWNBEARD
Verbesina encelioides, likes full sun. Blooms spring to early fall. Grows 1-3' tall. Low water use. Annual.

MID BLOOM

EASTERN PURPLE CONEFLOWER
Echinacea purpurea, likes full sun/ partial shade. Blooms late spring to early summer. Grows 2-3' tall. Medium water use. Perennial.

INDIAN BLANKET
Gaillardia pulchella, likes full sun. Blooms in the summer. Grows 1-1.5' tall. Medium water use. Annual.

WILD BERGAMOT
Monarda fistulosa, likes full sun/ partial shade. Blooms in the summer. Grows 2-4' tall. Medium water use. Perennial.

BASKET-FLOWER
Centaurea americana, likes full sun. Blooms in the summer. Grows 3-4' tall. Medium water use. Perennial.

MAXIMILIAN SUNFLOWER
Helianthus maximiliani, likes full sun. Blooms in the summer. Grows 3-10' tall. Medium water use. Perennial.

BLAZINGSTAR
Liatris punctata, likes full sun. Blooms in the summer. Grows 1-2' tall. Medium water use. Perennial.

LATE BLOOM

AROMATIC ASTER
Symphyotrichum oblongifolium, likes full sun. Blooms late summer to fall. Grows 2' tall. Drought tolerant. Perennial.

SHOWY GOLDENROD
Solidago speciosa, likes full sun. Blooms late summer to fall. Grows 2-3' tall. Medium water use. Perennial.

BLUE SAGE
Salvia azurea, likes partial shade. Blooms late summer to fall. Grows 3-6' tall. Medium water use. Perennial.

Photo provided by: Okies for Monarchs

Study nature, love nature, stay close to nature.
It will never fail you.
—Frank Lloyd Wright, American architect

I often hear people say they don't want to use native plants for fear the neighbors won't approve, because it might look messy or violate their homeowner association guidelines. This is not the intent of this book. As landscape architects, we believe that every landscape, whether it's around your home or in a public space, should be gorgeous and fit right in with the surroundings. So, while creation of a prairie might work in some cases, there is absolutely nothing that says native plants must be messy.

Using native plants in our landscapes can simply mean that instead of using plants from other parts of the world, we use native plants in an ornamental way.

What does that mean? Instead of opting for introduced plants, or those that are not native to an ecosystem, we can achieve the same effect by choosing native plants. For example, consider these substitutions:

Traditional Alien Species	Consider this Native Plant
Mums (Asia, northeastern Europe)	Asters
Moneywort (Europe)	Purple Poppy Mallow
Autumn Joy Sedum (Europe, Asia)	Joe Pye Weed
Daylily (Asia)	Black-Eyed Susan
Vinca (Europe, southern Russia)	Frogfruit
Fountain Grass (Africa)	Blue Grama
Maiden Grass (Asia)	Switchgrass
Feather Reed Grass (Europe, Asia)	Indian Grass
Canna (Central America)	Giant Coneflower
Purple Leaf Euonymus (China, Japan, Korea)	Wild Strawberry
Liriope (China and Japan)	Gray Sedge

While this book focuses on forbs and grasses, the same approach works even better with trees and shrubs, which are equally important to our pollinators. So, instead of the alien species, consider these:

Traditional Alien Species	Consider this Native Plant
Chinese Pistache (China)	Kentucky Coffeetree
Lacebark Elm (China)	Cedar Elm
Goldenrain Tree (China, Japan, Korea)	Smoketree
Nellie R. Stevens Holly (Hybrid)	American Holly
Austrian Pine (Western Europe)	Canaert Juniper
Weeping Willow (China)	Bald Cypress
London Planetree (Hybrid)	American Sycamore
Japanese Barberry (China, Japan)	Common Ninebark
Crape myrtle (Philippines, Japan, China)	Red Yucca
Boxwood (Europe, Asia)	Dwarf Yaupon Holly
Rose (Asia)	Autumn Sage
Pyracantha (Europe)	Beautyberry

There are many more examples of native plants that work equally well. While providing the same beauty, shade, structure in the landscape, native plants also provide environmental support to wildlife that might be desperately needing food, shelter and habitat.

Ideally, the entire landscape design process, which involves the selection of plants to fit a specific location, will shift to prioritize native plants in our landscapes.

Watching something grow is good for morale. It helps us believe in life.
- Myron Kaufmann

In Oklahoma, one of the biggest challenges for large-scale planting projects is the prevalence of Bermuda Grass. This invasive species, introduced from Africa back in the 1800's, has firmly established itself as the dominant turfgrass in full sun locations statewide. It continues to be planted along every roadway, park, and residential or commercial development – unless someone specifically requests that it be removed. Bermuda grass does offer an important value to the landscape; it establishes quickly, prevents erosion, and spreads through Oklahoma's driest summers and deepest freezes. It will probably always be with us as a dominant turf grass.

However, when preparing an area for new plantings, it is important to kill or remove the Bermuda Grass first. While organic methods like solarization, smothering, or digging it out can work in small garden spaces, their effectiveness is limited when tackling medium to large-scale projects, based on my experience.

My recommendation for successful Bermuda grass removal requires at least two applications of herbicide to create a clean growing area. Ideally, an herbicide containing glyphosate, such as Roundup, should be applied during the late summer when the grass is green and actively growing. It's crucial to follow label instructions and to prevent overspray onto any plants to remain. After 2-3 weeks, reapply the herbicide to eliminate any remaining green grass. The dead grass can be left in place to serve as a natural mulch. The roots help to prevent soil erosion while new plants are being established.

Once the area is planted, the likelihood of new Bermuda Grass growing goes down. The newly established vegetation provides shade and the one condition that Bermuda doesn't grow in is shade.

Once the removal of invasive grass and weeds is complete, it is time to plant. There is always a debate about when is the best time to plant. Both the fall and springtime have advantages as well as disadvantages:

Fall Planting: If done in fall, the plants have a great chance to become established before they need to produce new top growth and endure the heat of summer. Roots grow through the winter months, preparing the plant for spring. Fall is definitely the best time to plant trees and woody plants for that reason. Herbaceous plants will also perform better if planted in the fall.

There are two reasons you may need to wait for spring:

1. Frequently, there are usually both fewer plants and a smaller selection of plants that are available in the nursery trade for fall planting. Also, plants can be picked over by fall, so those that are left are not the best quality.
2. You don't want to forget where your plants are. Many forbs and grasses will die to the ground in the fall and be covered by leaves or mulch. Come spring, when you are ready to see plants grow, you may have lost them and plant something else in its place. (I regret that I have learned this the hard way!) Be sure to mark new plants with stakes, or on a plan that you can refer to in the spring.

Spring Planting: If planting in the spring, aim to plant as soon as plants break dormancy and become commercially available. Grasses and forbs seem to be ready to burst into growth in spring, and you want to be sure they are in the ground when they are ready. If you can get plants in the ground before or as the first flush of growth begins, you will see some real growth in the first year.

Ideally, you should plant an entire garden area at once; including trees, woody plants, forbs and grasses. This makes it easier to arrange plants properly, ensuring each plant getting the space it needs to grow.

When placing plants, work from those that will get the largest down to the smallest for best results.

Planting one area at a time also helps with maintenance. You will know to where to watch for weeds and where to add needed water during the first year.

Planting at other times: We've all experienced the irresistible urge to add that perfect plant to our landscape immediately. I've done it a thousand times and say, "Go for it!" As long as it isn't 100 degrees in the shade, or in the middle of a spring monsoon, it is good for the soul to keep adding to our gardens. Do your best to plant properly and to add extra water if needed.

Plant Sizes

Most of the plants in this book are intended to be planted as container plants rather than seed. One of the many great things about native plants is that you don't need to plant very large plants. A one-gallon plant will usually fill a spot within the first year. For smaller plants where spacing will be close together, four-inch pots or even plugs will work just fine, since native plants tend to be more tolerant of drought and other weather extremes, even when small. This not only saves you money but also allows you to plant more of your landscape at a time.

Seeding

Another way to establish native plants is by seed. Although sometimes slower, it is a much less costly way to plant large areas and some species are only available by seed. Preparation of the planting area, especially removing Bermuda grass, remains important. Timely planting, usually fall for perennials and native annuals, and spring for grasses, is essential.

There are several native wildflower and grass seed mixes available, or even better, you can buy individual species that are appropriate for your site. Custom mixes can be created by some seed companies for larger sites. Be sure to plant seed at the proper depth and with good seed to soil contact. Make sure to water the newly seeded areas for good germination and establishment. Locally sourced seed is more likely to adapt and is recommended for better success rates.

Soil

When selecting plants for your garden, be sure that they are compatible with the soil conditions of your site, as noted in each of the plant profiles. It is important to resist the urge to amend the soil with fertilizer, as rich soils tend to make native plants grow taller only to then flop over.

Unsure if your soil is sandy, clay, or a perfect loam? Here is a simple test: wet your soil slightly, then take a bit in your hand and roll it into a ball or ribbon. If it doesn't hold its shape, you have sandy soil. If it holds together nicely, you have clay. If it is somewhere in between, you are one of the lucky few with loamy soil.

Maintenance

A native landscape can be maintained much like any other landscape, but with several major advantages:

1.   Less watering

The majority of the plants in this book have evolved to be tolerant of the drought conditions that are normal in an Oklahoma summer. While some initial watering for establishment might be necessary, I've found that more plants of all types are killed by overwatering than underwatering.

Now, I will confess that I am not a waterer. There are so many better things to do with my time and money. Even though my house came with an irrigation system, I seldom use it. Yes, I have occasionally lost plants to drought, but not often. Those plants just weren't meant to be in my life. I want the toughest plants and that is one reason why I love native plants so much.

If you are one who's therapy is watering plants, choose them carefully.

Watch plants carefully for the first couple of years. You will probably only need to water during extreme drought events. After that, they are best left alone. When you're tempted to water your plants, instead of doing it automatically, reach down and feel the ground to check the moisture level of the soil. Native plants are known for their deep root systems, often extending several feet down into the soil and reaching water that may not be available to other plants.

2.   No fertilization

If grown in too rich of a soil, native plants can grow too tall and flop over when flowering.   Adding fertilizer actually can make native plants less healthy and less attractive.

3.   In the fall: leave the leaves.

The eggs of many insects, including bees and butterflies are laid in those leaves and they use them for protection during hibernation. Embrace a nature-friendly approach and let this free natural mulch remain on the ground through the winter. Don't mow them, and certainly don't bag them for the landfill. Just take it easy in the fall, enjoy the colors and cooler temperatures and just leave them be.

Commercial mulch will rob the soils of nitrogen as it decomposes, plus it costs a lot!	*Fallen leaves makes a great free mulch, and leaving them preserves the eggs of the pollinators.*

4.   Also, leave seedheads

Those seeds are food for the birds during the winter. The seeds of Sunflowers, Coneflowers, Black Eyed Susans, Bee Balm and Ironweed are great for feeding the birds. The plants will hold on to their seeds through the winter, adding winter interest to your landscape. Seed-eating birds such as finches, chickadees, juncos, and sparrows rely heavily on this food source and the shelter provided by the seedheads to survive and thrive until the spring thaw.

5.   Save the stems

In the spring, most people want to neaten things up a bit to get ready for the big flush of growth. Remember this is a *spring event* If grasses and top growth are cut in the fall, the insulating value of that top growth is lost and plants can be exposed to a hard killing freeze. (I see people cutting things down in the fall all of the time and don't understand it!)

When you do cut the stems in the spring, don't cut all the way to the crown. It is important to leave 8-12 inches of stems that might still be harboring the hibernating bees. Leaving as much of those stems on the ground can serve as a mulch around the plants, enriching the soil and holding in moisture.

Stems of grasses and forbs provide nesting places for bees. They can be left on the ground and used as a free mulch.

6.   Don't spray to kill insects

Doing this will also kill the pollinators that we are trying to support. Even as you see caterpillars eating your milkweed, resist the impulse to "save" the plant. Insects and caterpillars will almost never actually kill a plant. Remember that is what the plants are for.

To summarize: maintenance of a native landscape mostly involves having a nice glass of tea on your porch while you watch nature at its best. OK, maybe I exaggerate! Your actual maintenance tasks will consist of weeding, much like any other landscape. You will notice that by the second spring, as the plants naturally expand, either through seed or growth, they will prevent much of the weed establishment, minimizing this task over time.

*Flowers always make people better, happier, and more
helpful; they are sunshine, food and medicine for the soul.*
—**Luther Burbank**

One of the main reasons people resist planting natives is that they
fear the neighbors will complain. If you have a messy, unkempt landscape,
whether planted with natives or not, they may have a right to do so. A
native plant landscape is not synonymous with a messy one. Here are a
few tips:

1. Design your landscape thoughtfully, following the same principles
   as with non-native plants: selecting the right plant for the right
   place.
2. Hide some of the "messy" parts of native plants, by arranging
   them so leggy parts are hidden by lower growing grasses or
   shorter plants.
3. Combine plants with different flowering times so there is always
   something blooming and beautiful to look at.
4. Keep edges neat! Keep plants low or trimmed next to sidewalks
   and roadways. Use a mow strip, stone, or steel edging to define
   planting area edges in a pleasant design. Keep the outside of
   those edges trimmed or mowed to contrast with the planting
   areas.
5. I've seen people who place signs in their yards to identify them
   as pollinator-friendly habitats. While I personally feel like these
   signs can detract from the overall garden effect, if it helps to
   educate your neighbors on how you are helping to save
   pollinators, then it might be worthwhile to place a tasteful sign in
   your yard.

PLANT SELECTION GUIDE

COMMON NAME	BOTANICAL NAME
FORBS	
COMMON YARROW	ACHILLEA MILLEFOLIUM
NODDING ONION	ALLIUM CERNUUM
LEADPLANT	AMORPHA CANESCENS
ARKANSAS BLUESTAR	AMSONIA HUBRICHTII
BLUESTAR	AMSONIA TABERNAEMONTANA
PRAIRIE PUSSYTOES	ANTENNARIA NEGLECTA
COLUMBINE	AQUILEGIA CANADENSIS
TEXAS GOLD COLUMBINE	AQUILEGIA CHYSANTHA VAR HINKLEYANA
ANTELOPE-HORNS	ASCLEPIAS ASPERULA
SWAMP MILKWEED	ASCLEPIAS INCARNATA
COMMON MILKWEED	ASCLEPIAS SYRIACA
BUTTERFLY WEED	ASCLEPIAS TUBEROSA
WHORLED MILKWEED	ASCLEPIAS VERTICILLATA
GREEN MILKWEED	ASCLEPIAS VIRIDIS
BLUE FALSE INDIGO	BAPTISIA AUSTRALIS
YELLOW WILD INDIGO	BAPTISIA SPHAEROCARPA
CHOCOLATE DAISY	BERLANDIERA LYRATA
PURPLE POPPY MALLOW	CALLIRHOE INVOLUCRATA
TALL POPPY MALLOW	CALLIRHOE LEIOCARPA
BLUE MIST FLOWER	CONOCLINIUM COELESTINUM
LANCELEAF COREOPSIS	COREOPSIS LANCEOLATA
PLAINS COREOPSIS	COREOPSIS TINCTORIA
TALL COREOPSIS	COREOPSIS TRIPTERIS
THREADLEAF COREOPSIS	COREOPSIS VERTICILLATA
WHITE PRAIRIE CLOVER	DALEA CANDIDA

Full Sun	Part Sun	Shade
6+ hours	4-6 hours Full Sun, or dappled all day	Less than 4 hours, morning preference
Note: The Plant characteristics above are variable depending on		
weather, maintenance provided, and soil conditions		

EXPOSURE			SOILS			PLANT HEIGHT	POLLINATORS		TYPE	AGGRESSIVE INDICATOR
●	●		●	●	●	1-3'	●		PERENNIAL	HIGH
●	●		●	●	●	1-2'	●		PERENNIAL	MEDIUM
●	●		●	●		2-3'	●		PERENNIAL	LOW
●	●				●	2-3'	●		PERENNIAL	LOW
●	●				●	1'	●		PERENNIAL	LOW
●	●		●			<1'	●	●	PERENNIAL	MEDIUM
	●	●			●	1-3'		●	PERENNIAL	MEDIUM
	●	●		●		1-3'		●	PERENNIAL	MEDIUM
●			●			1-2'	●		PERENNIAL	LOW
●	●		●		●	3-4'	●	●	PERENNIAL	LOW
●					●	5'	●	●	PERENNIAL	HIGH
●			●	●		1-2'	●	●	PERENNIAL	LOW
●	●		●	●		1-3'	●	●	PERENNIAL	MEDIUM
●			●	●	●	1-2'	●		PERENNIAL	MEDIUM
●	●		●	●		3-4'	●		PERENNIAL	LOW
●	●		●	●		3-4'	●		PERENNIAL	LOW
●	●		●	●		1-3'	●	●	PERENNIAL	MEDIUM
●	●		●	●	●	1'	●	●	PERENNIAL	MEDIUM
●	●		●	●	●	2-3'	●	●	ANNUAL	MEDIUM
●	●	●	●	●	●	1-3'	●	●	PERENNIAL	MEDIUM
●	●		●	●	●	1-2'	●	●	PERENNIAL	MEDIUM
●	●		●	●	●	2-4'	●	●	ANNUAL	MEDIUM
●	●		●	●		3-6'	●	●	PERENNIAL	MEDIUM
●	●		●	●		1-3'	●	●	PERENNIAL	LOW
●					●	1-3'	●		PERENNIAL	LOW

Dry Soil	Medium Soil	Wet Soil	Attractive to Insects	Attractive to Birds
Sandy, Rocky	Rich, Well Drained	Clay or Holds Water	Provides Food	Provides Food

COMMON NAME	BOTANICAL NAME
PURPLE PRAIRIE CLOVER	DALEA PURPUREA
PALE PURPLE CONEFLOWER	ECHINACEA PALLIDA
PURPLE CONEFLOWER	ECHINACEA PURPUREA
CUTLEAF DAISY	ENGELMANNIA PINNATIFIDA
HORSETAIL	EQUISETUM HYEMALE
RATTLESNAKE MASTER	ERYNGIUM YUCCIFOLIUM
SNOW ON THE MOUNTAIN	EUPHORBIA MARGINATA
SWEET JOE PYE WEED	EUTROCHIUM PURPUREUM
WILD STRAWBERRY	FRAGARIA VIRGINIANA
COMMON BLANKETFLOWER	GAILLARDIA ARISTATA
INDIAN BLANKET	GAILLARDIA PULCHELLA
ROSE VERBENA	GLANDULARIA CANADENSIS
NARROW-LEAF SUNFLOWER	HELIANTHUS AUGUSTIFOLIUS
MAXIMILIAN SUNFLOWER	HELIANTHUS MAXIMILIANI
FALSE SUNFLOWER	HELIOPSIS HELIANTHOIDES
HEUCHERA, CORAL BELLS	HEUCHERA AMERICANA
HARDY HIBISCUS	HIBISCUS LAEVIS
TALL GAYFEATHER	LIATRIS ASPERA
PRAIRE BLAZINGSTAR	LIATRIS PYCNOSTRACHYA
DENSE GAYFEATHER	LIATRIS SPICATA
CARDINAL FLOWER	LOBELIA CARDINALIS
TURK'S CAP	MALVAVISCUS ARBOREUS
BLACKFOOT DAISY	MELAMPODIUM LEUCANTHUM
WILD BERGAMOT	MONARDA FISTULOSA
EASTERN BEE BALM	MONARDA BRADBURIANA

Full Sun	Part Sun	Shade
6+ hours	4-6 hours Full Sun, or dappled all day	Less than 4 hours, morning preference
Note: The Plant characteristics above are variable depending on		
weather, maintenance provided, and soil conditions		

EXPOSURE			SOILS			PLANT HEIGHT	POLLINATORS		TYPE	AGGRESSIVE INDICATOR
☀	◐	●	◇ (Dry)	◆ (Medium)	⬤ (Wet)		🦋	🐦		
●				●		1-3'	●		PERENNIAL	LOW
●	●			●		2-3'	●		PERENNIAL	MEDIUM
●	●	●	●	●	●	2-5'	●	●	PERENNIAL	MEDIUM
●	●	●	●	●	●	1-3'	●	●	PERENNIAL	MEDIUM
●	●	●	●	●	●	2-4'			PERENNIAL	HIGH
●			●	●	●	4-5'	●		PERENNIAL	MEDIUM
●			●	●		1-3'	●		ANNUAL	MEDIUM
●	●	●		●	●	5-8'	●	●	PERENNIAL	LOW
●	●	●	●	●	●	<1'	●	●	PERENNIAL	HIGH
●			●			<1'	●	●	PERENNIAL	HIGH
●			●	●		1-2'	●	●	ANNUAL	LOW
●			●	●		<1'	●	●	PERENNIAL	LOW
●	●		●	●	●	5-8'	●	●	PERENNIAL	HIGH
●	●		●	●	●	6-10'	●	●	PERENNIAL	HIGH
●			●	●	●	3-6'	●	●	PERENNIAL	HIGH
	●	●		●		1-2'	●	●	PERENNIAL	LOW
●				●	●	4-6'	●	●	PERENNIAL	LOW
●	●		●	●		2-3'	●	●	PERENNIAL	LOW
●	●		●	●		2-5'	●	●	PERENNIAL	LOW
●				●	●	2-6'	●	●	PERENNIAL	LOW
●	●				●	2-4'	●	●	PERENNIAL	LOW
●	●	●	●	●	●	3-6'	●	●	PERENNIAL	LOW
●			●			1'	●	●	PERENNIAL	LOW
●	●				●	2-4'	●	●	PERENNIAL	HIGH
●	●				●	1-2'	●	●	PERENNIAL	HIGH

◇	◆	⬤	🦋	🐦
Dry Soil	**Medium Soil**	**Wet Soil**	**Attractive to Insects**	**Attractive to Birds**
Sandy, Rocky	Rich, Well Drained	Clay or Holds Water	Provides Food	Provides Food

COMMON NAME	BOTANICAL NAME
GAURA	OENOTHERA LINDHEIMERI
MISSOURI EVENING PRIMROSE	OENTHERA MACROCARPA
GOLDEN RAGWORT	PACKERA AUREA
ROUNDLEAF RAGWORT	PACKERA OBOVATA
WILD QUININE	PARTHENIUM INTEGRIFOLIUM
FOXGLOVE BEARDTONGUE	PENSTEMON DIGITALIS
WILD BLUE PHLOX	PHLOX DIVARICATA
TALL GARDEN PHLOX	PHLOX PANICULATA
DOWNY PHLOX	PHLOX PILOSA
CREEPING PHLOX	PHLOX SUBULATA
FROGFRUIT	PHYLA NODIFLORA
SMOOTH SOLOMON'S SEAL	POLYGONATUM BIFLORUM
SLENDER MOUNTAIN MINT	PYCNANTHEMUM TENUIFOLIUM
MEXICAN HAT	RATIBIDA COLUMNIFERA
BLACK-EYED SUSAN	RUDBECKIA FULGIDA
BLACK-EYED SUSAN	RUDBECKIA HIRTA
BLACK-EYED SUSAN	RUDBECKIA MISSOURIENSIS
GIANT CONEFLOWER	RUDBECKIA MAXIMA
SWEET CONEFLOWER	RUDBECKIA SUBTOMENTOSA
BLUE SAGE	SALVIA AZUREA
AUTUMN SAGE	SALVIA GREGGII
HOARY SKULLCAP	SCUTELLARIA INCANA
CUP PLANT	SILPHIUM PERFOLIATUM
BLUE-EYED GRASS	SISYRINCHIUM ANGUSTIFOLIUM
GOLDENROD	SOLIDAGO

Full Sun	Part Sun	Shade
6+ hours	4-6 hours Full Sun, or dappled all day	Less than 4 hours, morning preference
Note: The Plant characteristics above are variable depending on		
weather, maintenance provided, and soil conditions		

EXPOSURE			SOILS			PLANT HEIGHT	POLLINATORS		TYPE	AGGRESSIVE INDICATOR
☀	⛅	🌑	Dry	Medium	Wet		🦋	🐦		
●				●	●	2-4'	●		PERENNIAL	LOW
●				●	●	1'	●	●	PERENNIAL	HIGH
●	●	●			●	1-2'	●		PERENNIAL	HIGH
●	●	●			●	<1'	●		PERENNIAL	HIGH
●	●				●	1-3'	●		PERENNIAL	MEDIUM
●	●		●	●	●	3-5'	●	●	PERENNIAL	LOW
	●	●			●	1'	●	●	PERENNIAL	MEDIUM
●	●			●	●	2-4'	●	●	PERENNIAL	MEDIUM
●	●		●			1-2'	●		PERENNIAL	MEDIUM
●				●		<1'	●		PERENNIAL	LOW
●	●		●	●	●	1-2'	●		PERENNIAL	HIGH
	●	●			●	2-3'	●	●	PERENNIAL	MEDIUM
●	●		●	●	●	2-3'	●	●	PERENNIAL	MEDIUM
●			●	●		1-3'	●		PERENNIAL	MEDIUM
●	●		●	●	●	3-4'	●	●	PERENNIAL	MEDIUM
●	●		●	●	●	3'	●	●	ANNUAL	MEDIUM
●	●		●	●	●	2-3'	●	●	PERENNIAL	MEDIUM
●	●		●	●	●	5-7'	●	●	PERENNIAL	LOW
●	●			●	●	5-7'	●	●	PERENNIAL	MEDIUM
●	●		●	●		3-5'	●	●	PERENNIAL	LOW
●			●	●		1-3'	●	●	PERENNIAL	LOW
	●	●	●	●	●	2-3'	●	●	PERENNIAL	MEDIUM
●					●	4-8'	●	●	PERENNIAL	HIGH
●	●			●		<1'	●		PERENNIAL	LOW
●			●	●		2-6'	●	●	PERENNIAL	HIGH

🝆	🝆	🝆	🦋	🐦
Dry Soil	**Medium Soil**	**Wet Soil**	**Attractive to Insects**	**Attractive to Birds**
Sandy, Rocky	Rich, Well Drained	Clay or Holds Water	Provides Food	Provides Food

COMMON NAME	BOTANICAL NAME
NEW ENGLAND ASTER	*SYMPHYOTRICHUM NOVAE-ANGLIAE*
AROMATIC ASTER	*SYMPHYOTRICHUM OBLONGIFOLIUM*
SPIDERWORT	*TRADESCANTIA OHIENSIS*
SPIDER LILY	*TRADESCANTIA VIRGINIANA*
GOLDEN CROWNBEARD	*VERBESINA ENCELIOIDES*
NARROWLEAF IRONWEED	*VERNONIA LETTERMANNII*
GOLDEN ALEXANDER	*ZIZIA AUREA*

GRASSES	
BIG BLUESTEM	*ANDROPOGON GERARDII*
BUSHY BLUESTEM	*ANDROPOGON GLOMERATUS*
SIDEOATS GRAMA	*BOUTELOUA CURTIPENDULA*
BUFFALO GRASS	*BOUTELOUA DACTYLOIDES*
BLUE GRAMA	*BOUTELOUA GRACILIS*
PLAINS OVAL SEDGE	*CAREX BREVIOR*
GRAY'S SEDGE	*CAREX GRAYI*
PENNSYLVANICA SEDGE	*CAREX PENNSYLVANICA*
TEXAS SEDGE	*CAREX TEXENSIS*
NORTHERN SEA OATS	*CHASMANTHIUM LATIFOLIUM*
PURPLE LOVE GRASS	*ERAGROSTIS SPECTABILIS*
PINK MUHLY GRASS	*MUHLENBERGIA CAPILLARIS*
ROSE MUHLY GRASS	*MUHLENBERGIA REVERCHONHI*
MEXICAN FEATHER GRASS	*NASSELLA TENUISSIMA*
SWITCHGRASS	*PANICUM VIRGATUM*
LITTLE BLUESTEM	*SCHIZACHYRIUM SCOPARIUM*
INDIAN GRASS	*SORGHASTRUM NUTANS*
PRAIRIE DROPSEED	*SPOROBOLUS HETEROLEPIS*

Full Sun	Part Sun	Shade
6+ hours	4-6 hours Full Sun, or dappled all day	Less than 4 hours, morning preference
Note: The Plant characteristics above are variable depending on		
weather, maintenance provided, and soil conditions		

125

EXPOSURE			SOILS			PLANT HEIGHT	POLLINATORS		TYPE	AGGRESSIVE INDICATOR
☀	◐	✹	◇	◆	⬤		🦋	🐦		
●	●		●	●	●	3-5'	●		PERENNIAL	MEDIUM
●	●		●	●		2-4'	●		PERENNIAL	MEDIUM
●	●		●	●	●	2-3'	●	●	PERENNIAL	LOW
	●	●	●	●	●	1-3'	●	●	PERENNIAL	LOW
●				●		1-4'	●	●	ANNUAL	HIGH
●	●			●	●	2-3'	●		PERENNIAL	LOW
●	●		●	●	●	1-3'	●		PERENNIAL	LOW
●			●	●	●	5-8'	●		PERENNIAL	HIGH
●					●	2-4'	●	●	PERENNIAL	HIGH
●			●	●	●	1-2'	●	●	PERENNIAL	HIGH
●					●	<1'	●		PERENNIAL	HIGH
●			●	●	●	1-2'	●	●	PERENNIAL	MEDIUM
●	●		●	●	●	1'	●		PERENNIAL	MEDIUM
●	●				●	2-3'	●		PERENNIAL	MEDIUM
	●	●	●			<1'	●		PERENNIAL	MEDIUM
●			●	●	●	1'	●		PERENNIAL	MEDIUM
	●	●	●	●	●	2-3'	●	●	PERENNIAL	HIGH
●	●		●	●	●	1-2'	●	●	PERENNIAL	HIGH
●				●		2-4'		●	PERENNIAL	LOW
●			●	●		2-3'		●	PERENNIAL	LOW
●			●	●	●	1-3'		●	PERENNIAL	HIGH
●	●		●	●	●	3-8'	●	●	PERENNIAL	MEDIUM
●	●		●	●		2-4'	●	●	PERENNIAL	MEDIUM
●	●		●	●	●	3-8'	●	●	PERENNIAL	LOW
●				●		2-3'		●	PERENNIAL	LOW

◇	◆	⬤	🦋	🐦
Dry Soil	**Medium Soil**	**Wet Soil**	**Attractive to Insects**	**Attractive to Birds**
Sandy, Rocky	Rich, Well Drained	Clay or Holds Water	Provides Food	Provides Food

In the spring, at the end of the day,
you should smell like dirt.
—Margaret Atwood
Novelist, Poet, Environmental Activist

Native Plants Q & A

Question: What is difficult about landscaping with native plants?

Answer: Finding them! Luckily, several Oklahoma growers specialize in native plants and there are more growers all of the time. Planting with natives is a growing trend, and these plants are gradually making their way into garden centers across the state. However, due to the relatively low commercial demand, they might not grow the variety and quantity to supply what is needed in any given year. So, one year, you might fall in love with Rudbeckia maxima, and the next, you might not be able to find the plant for sale.

In 2023, the Oklahoma Native Plant Network (ONPN) was formed to address this problem. Their combined mission is to educate the public on the reasons to plant native plants, and to educate and encourage more growers to propagate and sell natives.

Check with both the Oklahoma Native Plant Society and the Oklahoma Native Plant Network websites for a listing of local growers.

Question: How does a gardener deal with that?

Answer: Stay flexible. Be prepared to substitute similar plants if needed, or plan ahead by placing orders in advance. The likelihood of finding the plants you want improves if you contact your favorite growers four or six months in advance of when you want them. That works best when you are needing a lot of plants, but it can help even the average gardener.

Question: What about ordering native plants by mail?

Answer: I highly encourage everyone to support local growers as a priority. We need them and we want them to succeed and grow more native plants. Years ago, I ordered plants through a catalog with a very poor outcome. The plants arrived smaller than expected and in various degrees of vigor. Ultimately, they did not survive. More recently, I ordered some Indian Grass online. The plants arrived on time and in good health. They were smaller than I would have liked, which means they needed more care at first, but they survived. However, please don't resort to catalog or online purchases just to save money. Order online only if plants cannot be found locally.

Plants that are grown in the same geographic area as where they will be planted have been proven to grow better than those brought in from far away. This is called 'provenance' which relates to a place of origin. It basically means that, if possible, purchase plants or seeds that have been propagated within 100 or 200 miles of the ultimate planting site. For instance, a Purple Coneflower that is grown in Oklahoma from an Oklahoma seed will be better adapted than one grown in California from a California seed. I don't mean to t pick on California; this goes for any far away state. This is not always possible, but something to consider when sourcing your plants.

Question: How long does it take for native plants to make a statement in a landscape?

Answer: There's only one good answer to that question: It depends—mostly, on when you plant. If plants are in the ground in March or April, when they begin to emerge from dormancy, you can expect to see an explosion of growth. Plants can fill in quickly—sometimes in a matter of weeks. Don't space plants too far apart; the goal should be to have the ground covered by the end of the first year so weeds and Bermuda Grass won't find themselves welcome. So, the short answer is you will see a big impact after the first growing season. In three years, you can expect a mature landscape.

Question: What else should I know?

Answer: Some plants will spread, reseed, and take over other plants. Such traits are alluded to in our plant descriptions and the Oklahoma plant selection guide. This can also happen with the introduced plants we grew up with. You can either weed them out or learn to love them, depending on the plant and your personality. The likelihood of how much a plant will spread relates to the growing conditions. Consider reducing irrigation or altering other maintenance practices if this becomes a problem. If you are a control freak, you may have a problem with some natives.

Question: What about gathering native plants from the wild?

Answer: No! Transplanting plants with deep root systems is difficult and will often result in the death of the plant. It also robs the wild of native plants. Leave this work to professionals.

Question: Do I need to get rid of my non-native plants?

Answer: No! Our goal is simply to encourage more people to use native plants as ornamentals. I am not about to remove all of my Junipers, Abelia, or the Japanese Boxwoods that have been growing on my property for years. Instead, I plant native plants in my new beds and use them to fill in around my old non-natives. If a plant dies, I look to native plant lists first for a replacement.

Question: Any more advice?

Answer: Yes, soil requirements are noted for each plant. This is more important on natives than your standard garden-center plant. If you have heavy red clay, you will have trouble growing something that wants well-drained soil. Remember to match the plant to the soil type.

*The glory of gardening: hands in the dirt, head in the sun,
heart with nature. To nurture a garden is to feed not just
the body, but the soul.*
- Alfred Austin

*I love spring anywhere, but if I could choose
I would always greet it in a garden.*
**-Ruth Stout
American gardening author**

More Plants to Try

Over the years, I made it my personal goal to try planting only natives in my home landscape. In this, I have mostly succeeded. I also wanted to try every native plant first hand, so that I have personal experience with them all. In this, I have failed. The more that I learn about, the more plants there are to try, and ultimately, I have given up. There are just too many!

In this book, we have featured native plants that we have personally used in Oklahoma. Along the way, however, we also received recommendations about other native plants that local growers have seen fare well here. I am looking forward to trying them. Until then, we share some of those suggestions in the following list, with the hope that you'll let us know if you find them a good addition to the repertoire of Oklahoma native plants.

Hymenoxys odorata, Bitter Rubberweed: An annual, native to the dry western parts of Oklahoma. This plant is low-growing with long blooming yellow flowers. It is poisonous to livestock and sheep.

Phlox stolonifera, Creeping Phlox: This plant looks very much like the Phlox subulata, but has purple flowers and grows in shade.

Rivina humilis, Pigeonberry: Another low-growing ground cover for the shady places in your landscape.

Verbesina alternifolia, Wingstem: Easy to grow from seed, this native plant grows four to eight feet tall with yellow blooms from August to October. It can be somewhat weedy but is good for naturalizing.

To make a prairie it takes a clover and one bee,
One clover, and a bee.
And revery.
The revery alone will do,
If bees are few.
- Emily Dickinson, American poet

Native plants grace public spaces across Oklahoma, providing gardeners the opportunity to see these plants in various settings – ranging from prairies to informal to formal. Here are a few places to see native plants in Oklahoma at their best, including one where they still grow wild.

Oklahoma City
Myriad Botanical Garden
301 W. Reno Avenue, Oklahoma City, OK 73102

Oklahoma State Capitol Complex
Various buildings, and the Memorial Grove, 2300 N. Lincoln Boulevard, Oklahoma City, OK 73105

Oklahoma City Zoo and Botanical Garden
2101 N.E. 50th Street, Oklahoma City OK 73111

Will Rogers Garden, Will Rogers Park
3400 N. W 36th Street, Oklahoma City OK 73112

Kirkpatrick Garden at OSU-OKC
400 N. Portland Avenue, Oklahoma City OK 73107

Martin Park Nature Center
5000 W Memorial Road, Oklahoma City OK 73142

Scissortail Park
300 S. W Seventh Street, Oklahoma City OK 73109

Tulsa
The Gathering Place
2650 S. John Williams Way E., Tulsa, OK 74114

Tulsa Botanic Garden
3900 Tulsa Botanic Drive Tulsa, OK 74127

Woodward Park: 2435 S. Peoria Avenue, Tulsa, OK 74114

Stillwater
The Botanic Garden at Oklahoma State University
3300 W Sixth Street, Stillwater, OK 74078

Pawhuska
Tallgrass Prairie Preserve
15316 County Road 4201, Pawhuska, OK 74056

Poteau
The Kerr Center for Sustainable Agriculture:
24456 Kerr Road Poteau, OK 74953

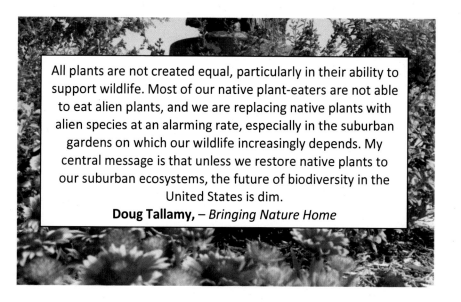

All plants are not created equal, particularly in their ability to support wildlife. Most of our native plant-eaters are not able to eat alien plants, and we are replacing native plants with alien species at an alarming rate, especially in the suburban gardens on which our wildlife increasingly depends. My central message is that unless we restore native plants to our suburban ecosystems, the future of biodiversity in the United States is dim.
Doug Tallamy, – *Bringing Nature Home*

American Society of Landscape Architects (ASLA): founded in 1899, professional association representing landscape architects worldwide.

alien, exotic or introduced: refers to a non-native plant species that are used in the landscape, typically originating from Europe, Japan, China, Africa, South America or other parts of the world. These plants can cause environmental harm or adversely impact biodiversity, by leading to the decline or elimination of native species.

annual: a plant that completes its life cycle within one year, before dying.

clay soil: soil with a high amount of clay, which sticks together when compressed, lacks oxygen, and fails to easily absorb water.

cultivar: plant variety produced in cultivation by selective breeding for developing special characteristics, such as flowering, fruiting, or size.

deadheading: to pinch or remove dead or faded flowers from plants, commonly done to increase flowering or improve appearance.

enriched soil: high-quality garden soil that has been enriched with compost, and or organic nutrients.

foliage: the aggregate of leaves of one or more plants.

herbaceous: plants, or herbs, that have no persistent woody stem.

hybrid: a hybrid plant is the result of cross pollinating two different plant varieties. This tends to be done to get 'improved' attributes of each plant into a new variety.

invasive plant: a plant that is usually an introduced species which is able to establish on many sites, grows quickly, and spreads to the point of threatening biological diversity or ecosystems.

legume: a family of plants with the ability to harvest nitrogen gas from the air and combine it with hydrogen, producing a form of nitrogen that can improve the soil and provide supplemental nitrogen to nearby plants.

mulch: a layer of organic material spread over the surface of soil to reduce evaporation, control weeds, regulate temperature, enrich soil, reduce erosion, and add beauty.

nativar: a cultivar of a native plant, generally done to select for improved flowering, color or other growth characteristics.

native plant: a plant that is a part of the balance of nature having developed for hundreds or thousands of years in a particular region or ecosystem.

naturalized: a non-native plant that does not need human help to reproduce and maintain itself over time in an area where it is not native.

ONPS, or the Oklahoma Native Plant Society was formed in 1987 with the purpose of encouraging the study, protection, propagation, appreciation, and use of the state's native plants. The society's varied activities promote an awareness and understanding of some of the state's most valued treasures. More at www.oknativeplants.org

ONPN, or the Oklahoma Plant Network was formed in 2023 to promote the use and commercial availability of native plants. Their goal is to engage the public in various ways to demonstrate the importance and benefits of using native plants in landscaping and land stewardship practices. More at www.onpn.org

perennial: a plant that persists for many growing seasons. Generally, the top portion of plant dies back each winter, and the plant regrows the following spring from the same root system. Some perennials do keep their leaves year-round and make for evergreen borders or ground covers.

pollination: the transfer of pollen between the male and female parts of flowers to enable fertilization and reproduction. Most plants depend on pollinators to transfer pollen.

pollinators: a group of animals—especially bees, flies, wasps, butterflies, moths, beetles, weevils, ants, midges, bats, and birds—that serve to pollinate plants.

rhizome: a continuously growing horizontal underground stem that sends out lateral shoots at intervals, allowing plants to spread.

Registered Landscape Architect (RLA): a landscape architect that has taken and passed the Landscape Architect Registration Examination and is licensed by the state to practice landscape architecture.

sedge: a grass-like plant with triangular stems and less conspicuous flowers.

shrub: a small to medium sized woody plant. Unlike herbaceous plants, shrubs will have woody stems above the ground.

species: a group of related organisms that share common characteristics and are capable of interbreeding.

tap root: a straight tapering root growing vertically downward and forming the center from which subsidiary rootlets spring.

weed: a native or non-native plant that is not valued where it is growing.

All gardening is landscape painting.
—William Kent, English architect

We wish to thank the following organizations for providing information and images for this book.

LADY BIRD JOHNSON WILDFLOWER CENTER
4801 La Crosse Avenue, Austin, TX 78739 I (512)-232-0100
www.wildflower.org

MISSOURI BOTANICAL GARDEN
4344 Shaw Boulevard, Saint Louis, MO 63110 I (314)-577-5100
www.missouribotanicalgarden.org

NOBLE RESEARCH INSTITUTE
2510 Sam Noble Parkway, Ardmore, OK 73401 I (580)-223-5810
www. noble.org

PLANT DATABASES
www.illinoisbotanizer. com, www.oklahomaplantdatabase.org
www.plants.usda.gov, www.nrcs.usda.org

Other helpful references include:
KERR CENTER FOR SUSTAINABLE AGRICULTURE
24456 Kerr Road, Poteau, OK 74953 (918) 647-9123
www.kerrcenter.com

OKIES FOR MONARCHS
www.okiesformonarches.org

COMMON NAME INDEX

FORBS

GRASSES

SCIENTIFIC NAME INDEX

FORBS

GRASSES

Connie Scothorn, RLA, ASLA, founded the landscape architectural firm of CLS & Associates in 1999 in Oklahoma City. She holds a bachelor's degree in horticulture-landscape design from Oklahoma State University and is a licensed landscape architect. She is a member of the American Society of Landscape Architects and a founding member of the Oklahoma Native Plant Network.

Brian Patric, RLA, ASLA, joined CLS & Associates in 2010 and has become a partner in the firm. He has a degree from Oklahoma State University and is licensed as a Landscape Architect. He is a member of the American Society of Landscape Architects and has many years of experience with native plants.

Scothorn and Patric previously co-authored "Oklahoma Native Plants, A guide to designing landscapes to attract birds & butterflies" in 2019, published by The Roadrunner Press. The book you are holding is an expanded version incorporating additional plants and gardening advice.

About CLS & Associates

CLS & Associates is an award-winning landscape architecture firm in Oklahoma City, which engages in a variety of projects across the state. These include streetscape development, park design, playgrounds and recreational design as well as landscape projects of all sizes. The use of native plants to improve aesthetic and ecological benefits to all landscape sites has become a foundation of CLS's design principles. Visit www.clsokc.com for more information.